The Broken Road Home

...a true story

Evie Gallagher

Chapter One

Nanna and Pappy

Most people do not remember being babies, but I do. I think I am only a few months old, and I am lying on my back looking up at the sky, which is partially obscured by the hood of my pram. I am waving a short chubby arm, and something shiny catches my young eyes. On my wrist is a golden baby bangle, and as I stare at this shining wonder a woman's face appears, and she is looking down at me, blocking out the sun. This lady had teeth missing, and shoulder length, brown curly hair. I tried to move my head to get back the feel of the warm sun, but something around my head and underneath my chin was getting twisted. It was my bonnet.

I found out when I was older, that the lady looking down into my pram was one of my auntie's. I never found out which auntie, as over time most of them had to have teeth removed, and they all took to dying their hair several different shades over the years.

I am a little older now, maybe two or three years. I am being bounced up and down upon my Nanna's knee. Nanna had deep orange, tight curly hair like Aileen Quinn from the 1982 film Annie. My nanna was singing a song to me, she was always singing and smiling at me.

My pappy is across the short living room, only a few feet away, and he is sitting in a rocking chair, before an old television set. My Pappy is loud and encouraging me to come to him. I wouldn't though, not before I have my "suckie, suckie" (my dummy dipped in his Guinness). He was a tall, lanky man, whom walked with a limp. He had short dark hair, that was greased back, and made his hair look shiny. He threw his head back in laughter, as I took my dummy out of my mouth, motioning for him to take it, and my nanna took it from me and proceeded to dip my dummy in his Guinness. I loved the taste of the funny dark ale with its creamy top.

My Nanna then put my dummy back in my mouth, and then Pappy crossed the short distance between us and picked me up from my nanna's knee, and placed me on top of a square wooden table, and he turned the music up on the stereo. I remember shaking my blonde curls and stamping my feet encased in shiny red leather strap shoes to the rhythm of some Scottish jig. Nanna and Pappy were clapping their hands and the room rang out with their laughter as they watched me stamping and twirling. I loved to dance on pappy's table. Sometimes I would get so dizzy, and sleepy, and often wake up in their big bed, only to still hear them singing away, in their Scottish burr's.

I used to love sitting on pappy's rocking chair, and I would quite often try to rock myself backward and forwards, even whilst standing up. I was doing that very thing one day when Nanny scooped me up, taking my place on the rocker, and placed me on her knee, and she began to brush my long platinum curls. I loved the feel of it, and I remember getting little goose bumps all over my arms.

I loved my toys, in particular, a little plastic horse carousel that played music, a toy turn dial telephone with a red squeaky nose, and a dolly with short blonde hair. I liked to sleep with the dolly in nana and pappy's bed, and I would take it out in a little toy pram, and push her around outside.

The red brick flats where nana and pappy lived were four of five stories high, and every level had long balconies. Nanny and pappy's flat was on the ground floor. There was a sort of square in the middle, and opposite there were more flats exactly the same.

My pappy would often take me to the other side of the flats where there was this big, black ship with big gold letters on it.

The ship was called the Cutty Sark. The Cutty Sark is a famous clipper and it was during the 1800s one of the fastest ships for a time.

I was fascinated with all the giant sails, and I would stare at them flapping high up in the wind. The ship faced the river Thames, and all along the harbor were decommissioned black cannon's on blocks, and cemented to the ground. Pappy would sit me atop the cannons, and I would watch all the ships passing through the Thames at high tide.

On the opposite side of the river was the famous canary wharf, filled with glittering skyscrapers that lit up at night. There was also a large concrete dome, and the dome was the entrance to a long tunnel that took you underneath the Thames all the way to the other side, where you would exit out through another dome.

I also remember Pappy carrying me in his long thin arms all the way up the road to his favorite pub Tonky's, as it was called at the time.

Tonky's wasn't a very big place, it had stained glass windows and a long winding bar, and towards the rear, there were lots of tables.

Pappy would sit at the bar for hours, drinking his pint of Guinness, whilst chatting to everyone he knew. sometimes he would go behind the bar and help the landlord to serve the customers.

I remember it was a bit of a dark and gloomy place, filled with tobacco smoke and sometimes it would sting my eyes and make me cough.

There was a big jukebox on the wall, and pappy would fill it for me with silver coins, and then stand me on the bar so that I could dance. Pappy would tell me when I was older that I was just like a little Shirley Temple.

He used to tell everyone in the bar that I was his "bonny wee lassie" as I sat on a bar stool beside him, legs swinging, stuffing my cheeks with crisps and salted peanuts.

When it was time to leave he would pick me up in his arms and

5

precariously stagger back down the road with me towards home, singing at the top of his lungs.

Chapter Two

In the Dark

I don't remember my mother or my father at all. Apparently it was because my mother kept taking me to live with Nanny and pappy quite a lot, and my dad would come home from work to find me gone, and he would have to keep driving to nanna and pappy's to get me back, and bring me home, so that we could all be together...which is why I think that I don't have any real memories of her until a little bit later in my life. I don't remember my dad either, but that's because they had broken up.

I awoke alone in the big double bed that I shared with my mother, and the room was dark. I didn't like being on my own in the dark. I slid myself down off the bed and opened the door into a long room that served as a living room and kitchen.

My mother was tidying up in the kitchen when she noticed me standing in the doorway in my nightie. I remember that she looked at me with a small frown, and said rather tersely "get back te yer bed, it's not morning yet".

"I can't sleep," I replied, still hovering in the doorway, not knowing what to do with myself.

"Well, you canny stay here. Yer uncle Brian is coming round, so get back te yer bed, NOW please." My mother emphasizing the "now".

I didn't want to go back in that room by myself, but I slowly turned around and went back into the room. I left the door open a little way so that I would have some light in the room. I climbed back up into the big bed and covered myself up underneath a blanket and sheet. I wanted to cry. I wanted my mother to cuddle me up as Nanna did. I missed nanna and pappy.

I heard a hard knock at the front door, and then my mother greeting a man, whom I assumed was Uncle Brian. I heard his deep baritone voice, and then my mother's throaty laughter. I then briefly saw her frame by the doorway just before she closed it, cutting off my small shaft of comforting light and leaving me once more in the darkness

I had never heard of Uncle Brian before, well not that I remembered anyway. I was a curious child, and so after a little while of lying there, I decided to go and see who Uncle Brian was

Once again I got out of the bed and felt my way for the door. I was a little afraid that the door would make noise, or that my mother would see the door opening, and tell me off. I held my breath and gingerly pushed down on the door handle. The door opened with the smallest of creaks, and I held it just enough to see through. I gently exhaled, and I peered through the slight crack. I couldn't really see much of anything, other than the kitchen at the far end of the room. I still had my hand on the silver handle, and as I went to open the door a little further it made a louder creek, but I saw a tall man with very dark skin and a halo of fuzzy black hair. This must be uncle Brian I thought. He was about to sit on the sofa, but when he saw me he paused himself halfway, looking a little startled for his eyes widened, but then he parted his big lips and smiled. His gums were bright pink, and his teeth a brilliant white.

My mother looked annoyed, but she didn't tell me off like I thought she would. Instead, she tried politely urging me back to bed. The man called uncle Brian told her to let me stay up, and so with a sigh from my mother, she told me to sit on the sofa and watch the TV.

I don't know how long that I sat up with them for, but I remember that Uncle Brian was drinking the same sort of beer that my mother was drinking. I don't remember what it was that I was watching on the TV, but I know that I couldn't hear anything because they were talking and laughing. It seemed to me that the more they drank, the louder they got.

I only remember Uncle Brian coming round a few times, after that time, and then he stopped altogether, and I never saw him again.

Chapter Three

A monster at the door

I enjoyed playing on the landing outside of our flat door and I would often sit on the wide staircase. On this particular day, I was trying to slide down the wooden banister, which began to curve around, about halfway down towards the large open entryway on the ground floor. This is exactly what I was doing when my mother opened the front door to our flat. She notified me excitedly that Derek was coming round, and that I was to listen for the main doorbell ringing.

I had no idea who Derek was, but knowing that it must have been a friend of hers I just nodded in agreement.

I don't remember having any friends myself, not my own age in any case. I mostly spent my time bouncing on the bed which I shared with my mother, coloring in, or playing like I was now on the staircase. My mother never really liked to go many places except the off license for her beers or to get shopping. I wished sometimes that she would take me to a park to play, or something. I remember thinking maybe her friend Derek could take me to the park, and I would maybe ask him.

As I was counting the steps on the stairs, a loud ring pierced the entryway. In my excitement to get to the door fast, I stumbled forwards and fell only a few steps short of the bottom. I wasn't hurt thankfully, and so I got up still eager to answer the door.

As I got closer I could see a dark outline behind the stained glass window in the top of the door. I hesitated a little bit, but then as I went to reach for the brass doorknob a gloved black leather hand shot through the wide letterbox, and it was moving around as if to grab for me. I screamed in terror. My heart was beating so fast and hard, and my little legs were trembling. My mother hearing the scream came out of the flat, and to the top of the stairs.

"What's wrong wi ye!?" she called out frantically.

"There is a monster, and it tried to grab me." I cried.

"It's Derek! he's no monster" she said laughing as she opened the door to him. My mother didn't know how wrong she was....

My mother said he was joking. He probably was, but I didn't find it funny, despite them having a good laugh about it. I decided that I didn't want to ask Derek if he would take me to the park.

As he sat down on the sofa, where Uncle Brian had once sat, he stared at me. He was shorter than Uncle Brian, and his skin was lighter, like mine and my mothers. He smiled at me with thin lips, whilst running a now un-gloved hand through his short brown hair. I remember thinking that I much preferred Uncle Brian, he had a nicer smile and he was funny. Derek looked serious, and a little older too.

My mother went to the kitchen to make him a cup of tea, and when her back was turned he began to slowly wave his gloves back and forth, all the while staring at me.

Chapter Four

Moving House

I didn't really see much of Derek after that, mainly because I was usually in bed asleep when he visited. Until one day when my mother asked me to sit down beside her, and Derek on the tweed sofa. They announced that they were getting married, and we would be moving into a nice new house with a garden.

I had no idea what getting married meant, but if we were moving I remember wondering if that meant that we no longer had to share a bathroom with other people.

"No.," my mother said laughing. "We will have our own bathroom, and our own bedrooms." She said smiling softly.

My mother began talking differently. She still had her Scottish accent, but it sounded posher like she was trying to sound like Derek. Derek was English you see. My mother was also not as drunk as she usually was, and she seemed to talk to me a little bit more, as opposed to just letting me get on with playing in a room by myself.

The house was three bedroomed mid terrace in Durrington, Sussex. My room faced the rear of the house. My mother and Derek shared the room in the middle, and there was a small bathroom, and an empty room at the front of the house.

The front door opened into a square living room, and beyond that was the kitchen, also perfectly square. There was a door, which lead into a small but neat back garden with a low wall separating the grass area. There was also a back gate which lead to a car park with some garages, as well as an alleyway.

The front of the house had a neat patch of grass and a grey concrete path which led out into a square of other houses. In the center of all the houses was a large concrete area, with lots of grass poking out from the slabs.

∞∞∞

I remember sitting in my brand new bedroom, which I had all to myself. My mother thought it was wonderful, but I was unsure as I had always shared a bed with someone, first my nanna and pappy, and then my mother. I know that I was happy to have a room all to myself.

I didn't see a lot of Derek still, and neither did my mother really, as he would leave early in the morning, and he wouldn't return home until after six o clock. I remember every time he got home he would put his briefcase down beside the front door.

Derek didn't smile at me a lot, but he did seem polite.. at first anyway...

Once we have moved into the house I remember beginning to feel a little uncomfortable around him. I knew he didn't like me playing in the same room as him with my toys, and he would look irritated if I was playing very animatedly or if I was making too much noise.

He was always telling me "to speak properly" and "don't chew with your mouth open"

My mother began giving me my dinner before Derek got home from work in the evening's, and she stopped letting me bring my toys downstairs. I had to keep them in my bedroom and play in there.

I began to feel as if I was doing everything wrong all of the time, and it made me feel really sad because I didn't understand what I was or wasn't supposed to do anymore.

∞∞∞

We all went for a short drive in the car one day, and it was to a big supermarket.

My mother had sometimes given me a basket to help her carry, or I would try and push the trolly.

I remember my mother giving me the shopping trolly, but warning me" to keep it straight and not hit anyone with it."

I could barely see over the baby seat part, but I managed well enough. I could hear Derek constantly muttering to himself everytime that I got to close to an aisle or another shopper.

My mother decided to peel off, and she disappeared off down another aisle from us to get something. I don't know what it was, and so I carried on going around the supermarket with Derek right beside me.

Quite suddenly I heard his sharp intake of breath, and he hissed at me "to watch where I was bloody going." Whilst placing his hand in a tight grip around the back of my neck.

It was painful, and I remember shrieking aloud. "ow! You're hurting me!"

"I'm not hurting you." he said lowly "You don't know what pain is. Now watch where you are going."

I didn't understand I didn't hit anyone or anything with the trolly, so why did he grab me and tell me off? I thought and began to cry.

"Stop sniveling. I didn't hurt you." He said and smiled as my mother came back.

"What's wrong with Evie?" she asked Derek.

I can't remember what he said to her exactly, but it was something along the lines of me being a maniac with the trolly, and almost hitting people... or something like that.

Chapter Five

Lone Adventures

I don't know how much time passed before my mother told me that she was going to have a baby and that I would have either a brother or a sister.

I didn't understand how she was getting a baby, but I was looking forward to having a brother or a sister.

∞∞∞

I remember that she began going to a Doctor's surgery, not very far from the house. I think it was because she was having a baby, but I'm not sure, but every time we went the Doctor would try to make me laugh and give me a sticker.

I would often ask my mother when she was going to see the Doctor again because I wanted to see him. He made me laugh, gave me praise, and even stickers! He made me feel like I was a good girl, and not a silly one as Derek had called me on a few occasions.

My mother told me that you only went to the Doctor if you were poorly, and had a cough, and so I began pretending to cough... a lot! And I told her that she should take me to see the Doctor because I had a cough.

My mother wasn't daft, and she knew that I was putting it on, and so I decided to take myself to see the Doctor, if she wasn't going to take me, then I was going by myself.

I don't remember which way it was, or how far that I had to walk now, but back then I did, as that's exactly where I ended up!

I was sat in a busy waiting room for what felt like forever. I got very bored waiting for the Doctor to call me in to see him, and so I began handing out pamphlets from a table to all the waiting patients. I did not notice anyone looking at me curiously, and I certainly did not notice when a policeman was standing by, watching me.

The last thing I remember from that day was when that nice policeman let me sit in the front of his police car, and let me direct him back to my house. I remember him giving me his car radio and letting me speak into the microphone. I told them that I had been waiting all day for the Doctor, and I asked if the Doctor was sick?

I don't remember getting out of the police car and being walked back to my mother, who apparently was frantic with worry.

The spare room at the front of the house was filling up with baby bottles, nappies, and all sorts. It was around this time that my mother had told me that I wasn't to have my dummy anymore. I remember being absolutely distraught, and begging her over and over to please give me back my dummy. But my mother was having none of it, and so once again I left the house and took myself off to the big supermarket where we went shopping to go and get myself a dummy. I knew they had dummies there. I had seen them!

I navigated the busy main roads, full of whizzing cars, to get to the supermarket. Once there I went straight to where the dummies were. I then selected the one I wanted, ripped it out of the packet, and popped it in my mouth! I walked out, navigating the busy main roads once more, and I made it home.

"Where did ye get that dummy?" my mother asked me a little later on.

"At the shop," I replied with a lisp, as I had my dummy in my mouth.

"What shop? When?" she looked alarmed.

"Where we go with the trolly."

"Jesus Christ!" she shouted, making me jump.

I remember thinking... "what was wrong with her? she didn't have to go out and get it!."

A short time later she took it away from me, and I was miserable again.

The next day I was playing in the front bedroom, surrounded by all these baby thing's, and I spotted them right on top of a chest of drawers... bottles!

I opened the box containing two baby bottles. I took off the teat, popped my finger in the open end and began sucking on it. It wasn't my dummy, but it would just have to do.

I was careful to hide it in my room, and not let her see me with it. That was until I got busted. My mother then told me to suck my thumb. It wasn't like my dummy, but I got used to it after a while, and I liked it better when I stroked my finger on my pillowcase.

Chapter Six

Smoke and tears

I don't think Derek knew about my escapades at the Doctor's or the supermarket, but if he did I didn't know about it.

Early one morning I woke up, and my mother was still in bed. I decided to go downstairs and play with a square wooden kitchen stool. I tipped it over and sat between its square frame, and pretend I was driving a bus. I decided my bus needed passengers and so I quickly ran upstairs, grabbed a handful of teddies, and ran back to the kitchen with them. I sat back in my pretend bus, with my teddies stuffed behind me. I soon got fed up with that though and I was really hungry.

My mum was still sleeping, and so I thought I would make myself some toast. I popped the bread in and waited for it to pop up, just like my mother did. I waited and waited until black smoke began billowing up from the toaster. I realized that I needed to get the toast out, but it just wouldn't come out, no matter how much I yanked on the lever. My idea was to get a butter knife from the drawer and pull it out. As soon as I put the knife in the toaster, making contact with the metal, there was a loud pop! I had blown the toaster up.

The alarm that always went off when my mother was cooking started with it's piercing beep! Beep! Beep!, over and over. I had to place my hands over my ears. The room was filled with this bluish acrid smoke that caught the back of my throat, and

I couldn't stop coughing. I heard my mother racing down the stairs, and then she began wafting a tea towel in the air, all over the place, until she gave up with that and opened up the back door. I watched as the smoke began steadily whooshing out of the door.

"What did you do?" she asked

I explained that the toast wouldn't pop up, at the same time that my eyes were stinging, pouring with tears from the smoke and coughing.

My mother's response was… "yer lucky ya never got a belt aff it"

I didn't dare ask for anything to eat, and it wasn't one of my brightest ideas.

That evening I was given my supper and then sent up to my room. I heard Derek get home a little after, and I could hear my mother's voice as she greeted him. She sounded nervous. After a little while, I was called downstairs. After Derek had finished with his evening meal, he shouted for me to come downstairs. He then asked me to stand in front of him, and to tell him what I did to the toaster.

I was afraid to say anything, and all the while his lips were pressed firmly together, waiting for me to answer him.

"I'm sorry," I said ever so quietly.

"Get up to your room! And do not come out unless you are told to. Got it?" he shouted angrily.

I remember my lip wobbling, and my mother looked sad, as if she wanted to intervene on my behalf, maybe to tell him that I didn't mean to do it, but she didn't. I knew I had done something naughty, but at the time I didn't think it was. I didn't mean to blow up the toaster.

∞∞∞

I was staring at a white wedding cake with a blue silk ribbon wrapped around's its base, and a small spray of blue flowers on the top. Blue was my mother's favorite color.

My mother entered the living room with her ash blonde hair a fluffy billow around her lightly made-up face. She was wearing a soft blue dress with white trim. I don't remember seeing Derek, and I do not remember their wedding. I am not sure if I was there, as that day I remember sitting with an elderly couple that lived next door. I think their names were Dorothy and Ernie.

My mother and Derek went on their honeymoon to Devon afterward, and I do not remember where I went whilst they were away. It was maybe with one of my aunts and cousins.

Chapter Seven

Goodbye little bird

Despite my mother's new married life she still drank and left me to my own devices a lot of the time. My mother would always keep the house spick and span, and have his meals ready every day for when he got home from work.

I still did not eat with them. Derek's new rules after they married were "children should be seen and not heard" and "don't speak unless spoken to" there were others, such as do not get my clothes or shoes dirty, make sure my room was always tidy. I was not allowed to put my elbows on the dinner table, I had to eat with my mouth closed and quiet. I was to eat whatever was put down in front of me, even if I didn't like it I would have to sit there and eat it until it was all gone. I was not allowed to question anything. If I was told to do something I had to do it quickly.

He would come into my room in the morning and check my bed to make sure that it was made correctly. I was also to be quiet when he was home. Oh, there were so many more rules. I used to think he just made them up as he went along.

Derek didn't appear to be an affectionate man, not to me anyway. He rarely said anything kind or gave any praise. He was like a tap, he could run hot, or run cold depending on whatever mood he would be in, at any given time.

Up to this point, I still didn't have any friends. I had never attended any nurseries or even a playschool. I often felt quite lonely, and I would often try to amuse myself by playing with toys or taking myself off for little walks about the houses and alleyways.

∞∞∞

One afternoon I went out the front to play and I saw some flowers, and I decided to pick some and give them to my mother when I came upon a little brown bird, and it looked sick. I ran back into the house as fast as I could to tell my mother, but she wasn't interested. She told me to "leave it, and don't touch it."

I felt sad and rather frantic. I wanted to help the little bird, but I didn't know what to do and I needed her to tell me what I should do.

I ran from my mother and got some soft yellow dusters from the cupboard beneath the kitchen sink. I then took off upstairs, and I found a spray can of something in the medicine cabinet on the wall beside the toilet. The medicine cabinet is where I knew my mother kept all the medicines. By the time I climbed down from the toilet I was breathless, but I didn't stop. I ran back out to the wounded little bird as fast as my little legs could carry me.

The poor helpless bird hadn't moved at all, but I saw it's little eyes blinking. I whispered "that it would be okay" and that "I was going to make it better again."

I wrapped it's a small body within the dusters and tried stroking it's soft little brown head with one finger. The little bird was looking at me, and then its eyes slowly closed and did not re-open.

I tried to rationalize in my mind what could I do? I knew if you were sick, you took medicine. I thought that if I could give it some medicine really quickly then it would come back to me, and so I tried spraying the small lifeless bird, thinking it was medicine.

A man came up beside me and asked me "what was I doing?"

So I told him I was "giving it medicine"

And the man replied, "not with a can of deodorant you're not."

Obviously, I had no idea what a can of deodorant was until I showed my mother what I had used. All I can think of now is, thank the good lord that little birdy was dead before I covered it in antiperspirant.

Several days had passed, and I was outside playing when I noticed that there was a little boy about the same age as me, moving into one of the houses with his parents. We didn't get chatting until the following day, and he told me that his mum had gotten him a paddling pool. I had no idea what a paddling pool was, so he told me to come to his back garden and see it. My mum was having one of her afternoon naps and, so I didn't think she would mind so off I went with him to see his paddling pool.

He told me that I couldn't go in the paddling pool with my dress on and that I had to take it off, and so I did. It was a hot day, and I enjoyed the feel of the cold water on my skin, and I was so happy frolicking in that paddling pool with the little boy, splashing each other, running out of it and jumping back in.

The sound of a lady shrieking to "get out of that paddling pool" completely startled me. Who was she talking to? Me, or the boy?

"That's my mum," said the little boy. He told his mother that I was his friend and that we wanted to play in the pool.

His mother looked crossly at me, and then told her son to go in, and told me to put on my dress and go home.

∞∞∞

I realized much later on in my life looking back, that it would have been very strange for this mother seeing some strange girl playing completely naked in their paddling pool, splashing her son in the face. I didn't understand at the time what I had done wrong or why she was so shocked. I understand now of course. For starters, I should have been introduced, and secondly, I should have owned a bathing costume, but since I had never been swimming I didn't think I owned a costume. My mother was never interested in anything like that and well as for Derek, he never offered to take me. Thirdly I had never had the conversation about privacy and protecting one's body, and if I had it probably may have saved me for what was to eventually happen, but I don't think so, not really, it's more of a helpless thought really, and I don't think it would have made a difference.

Chapter Eight

Big changes

I was with my mother and step-father looking around a three bedroomed end terrace house, with a bigger garden. Lancing at that time was a small village with a railway crossing, a few shops and a couple of pubs. My mother loved the house, and so Derek bought it. They decorated my room with carebear wallpaper, and I had matching bedding.

During the daytime as well as nighttime I could hear the railway crossing warning going dee-doo, dee doo, as the gates would come down blocking traffic for the trains to pass through the village. The trains made it difficult for me to sleep some nights, at least for a while until I had gotten used to it, and then it never really bothered me anymore.

I started school in September 1985 at the only village first and secondary school. I was unfortunate to have an old teacher Miss Beck, whom clearly hadn't moved with the times, as she was very Victorian in her teaching practices, and she was just like Derek. Miss Beck found me to be not very smart, and seriously lacking in social skills. She would often threaten to rattle our backsides on many occasions if we spoke during class, or for not following her instructions precisely. Miss Beck once made me sit under the class table with cellotape over my mouth for whispering to myself as I counted on my fingers for a sum. It didn't really bother me. I was used to her brash ways, as I said... she was another Derek.

I did tell my mother one day when she actually did rattle my backside. Miss Beck was only a small wiry teacher, but she had power behind that hand, so much so that it actually made my butt sting for a little bit.

My mother drunkenly shouted "How dare she! I'll smash her bloody headlamps in!"

The next day I informed Miss Beck that if she hit me again that my mother was going to come down to the school and smash her headlamps. Miss Beck had me transferred to a different classroom.

I will say that I was by no means an unruly child. I was actually quite introvert. Unlike most of the other kid's who seemed to instantly hit it off with each other, I found it more difficult as I was too shy and too slow. The other kids would laugh at me if I didn't understand something, despite being told over, and over, or if I got told off. I think the kid's laughter hurt me more than the teacher's comments.

I made friends with a girl in my class her name was Deborah. It was easy to make friends with her, because most of the other kids that laughed at me, avoided her. Deborah I didn't think had ever used a hairbrush, and she had a permanent snotty nose or lip. Deborah and I would sit on the field at playtimes, avoiding the busy playground. It turned out that Deborah was allergic to most things, and her mother would always give her a bunch of medicines, but they clearly didn't work.

Deborah was my first best friend, and I also learned very quickly that children could be just as cruel as adults.

∞∞∞

My mum soon began drinking in the local British Legion, and sometimes she would have a bit of a flutter in the betting shop next door.

On Sundays, Derek would join her, and as for me, they sent me off to enroll myself in the local Tabernacle Sunday school. I learned about God, and his son Jesus, and I read every inch of the Bible and learned many hymns. I was allowed to join the choir, and I began going twice per week. The vicar had never met my parents or ever seen them in his congregation. The Vicar would often send me home with notes, though I could never read his handwriting. My mother and Derek were not church-going people, and so they never watched me sing in the choir, but that didn't matter, as the Vicar explained to me that I was singing to God, and he could hear me.

∞∞∞

I started to realize at five and a half that it was pretty much up to me to look after myself from the day that I got this awful toothache, that wouldn't go away.

I was sent to the school nurse, and she told me that I could get one of my parents to pull it out with a piece of string tied around my bad tooth and the other end looped onto a door handle, and the idea was for someone to hold me steady whilst someone slammed the door, and my tooth would pop out! She laughed and said she was joking, but that was how teeth used to be pulled. Then she suggested that I should go to see the dentist. I asked her where the nearest dentist was, and after school, I took myself there on the way home. There was no way I would let anyone pull out my tooth with a bit of string attached to a door!

∞∞∞

I sat on a waiting room chair swinging my legs back and forth waiting for my turn. A young lady behind a desk kept glancing at me, and after a while, she asked me if I was waiting for someone. I explained that I needed the dentist to take out my sore tooth. The lady behind the desk looked at me as if I had two heads, and not one. After she composed her facial expression, she told me that I needed a parent to come with me, as they would need to sign some forms.

I dejectedly took myself home, but not before the lady handed me the forms. My mother was drunk and refused to take me to the dentist. Her remedy was to give me oil of cloves, put a pack of frozen peas on my face and to wait for it to drop out.

I lay awake all night with the throbbing pain, I cried and cried.

Derek kept yelling at me from the next room to "shut up whining, or he would give me something to whine about!"

The frozen cold peas went warm and soggy, and I muffled my cries under my pillow and duvet.

The next morning I asked my mum to sign the forms, and write a letter to tell them it's okay for the Dentist to help me, as that's how she communicated with the Vicar and the school. My mother agreed, and on the way to school, I dropped the forms and letter off at the dentist.

By the end of the day, I was in so much pain that I felt physically sick. I remember it made my ears and head hurt so bad too.

When I got to the Dentist's the receptionist insisted on calling my mother to double check that she was happy for me to have treatment. I didn't know the number so the same lady from the day before had to look it up in the phone book.

The next thing I know I'm in a big long chair, surrounded by strange metal instruments, and a big bright light, and the lady from reception, who held my hand.

The lovely dentist man gave me my first ever filling, and he told me to stay away from sweeties.

Chapter Nine

All on my own

Eleven days after my sixth birthday my little sister Lucy was born. My Nanna had also just recently passed away from cancer. Apparently, Nanna was at the time living with one of my aunts having left my Pappy. I didn't know why.

Lucy was born premature and my mother told me that she "weighed less than a bag of sugar." My mother had to have an extended stay in the hospital, and my sister was being closely monitored. I was sent to stay with another of my aunts and two cousins for a week until my mother returned home.

I did miss my mother, but I was satisfied that I now had two cousins to play with, and I really enjoyed that week. It was kind of like a holiday for me in a way.

When my mother came home Derek told me that, I"wasn't allowed to go near her, as she needed her rest."

It was then that I learned to cook for myself. I cooked myself burgers and chips, or chip and fish finger butties. It was no big deal I had watched my mother do it lots of times... I was even making cups of tea for my mother and doing the housework.

Eventually, Lucy was allowed to come home from the hospital. My mother seemed soberer and was getting back to her old routine, and she was taking good care of Lucy. I helped out of course by changing nappies, keeping an eye on her when my mother went to lie down for a while.

Lucy was so small and beautiful. I was very happy to have my sister home at last! and I couldn't wait until she was older so that we could play out.

Derek seemed excited and a lot happier too, in fact, I don't think I had ever seen him so happy.

∞∞∞

When Lucy was a couple of months old, Derek booked a holiday for us at a caravan park, and a couple of their friends were also joining us. This was to be my first ever holiday, and I was feeling really excited.

When we arrived Lucy was placed into a basket for me to watch over her, whilst everyone else unloaded the luggage from the cars. Afterward, everyone sat down on the long sofa area at the end of the caravan, sipping cups of tea. Well everyone except for my mum who was drinking her usual can of larger, which I now knew was called Holsten Pills.

Everyone was cooing over Lucy, and saying how tiny and lovely she was when Derek told me "to go and unpack my suitcase"

Once I was done I asked my mother" if I could have something to eat?"

I think that she was about to answer me when Derek cut in "No you can bloody wait till later." He said irritably.

I remember my tummy was growling. I didn't eat any breakfast that morning, as there wasn't time, and it was now well past lunchtime. I sat down on the floor next to my mother who was holding Lucy, and I stroked her tiny cheek, and she began to cry.

"Get off her!" Derek snapped at me.

"Lucy's been asleep the whole journey, and she just needs her bottle," my mother said, looking nervously at Derek, who was glaring at me still.

"I will get it for you." I offered to get up, wanting to be away from Derek. I just didn't understand what his problem was with me.

"No, you won't. I will go and get it." He said bitterly. "Why don't you just go off and play?" he asked as he went to go and get Lucy's bottle.

"I don't know where to go," I said a little sulkily, and he glared at me. I felt as if no one wanted me around. I felt this hard painful knot in my throat, as I sat there watching them all. What was wrong with me? what have I done? I was asking in my mind and trying so hard not to cry. I could feel everyone staring at me, waiting expectantly for me to do what? I didn't know.

I got up, turned around, and as I walked away I said: "It's not fair." and I took my dejected six-year-old self off to go sit on the caravan steps outside.

Less than a minute later, Derek came up behind me, grabbed my arm in a painfully tight grip and yanked me up into the air, taking me into the back bedroom of the caravan. My feet never touched the floor. I started to protest, but he clamped his hand over my face, muffling my cries. He then placed me on my feet, and put both of his hands around my throat, and began to squeeze. I was fighting for air, and so he let just enough go so that I could breathe.

His eyes were slightly pink, and he spat in my face as he spoke to me quietly through gritted teeth. "Why don't you just go away, and do as your fucking told! Give your mother some peace. Lucy is my daughter, got it!"

I felt something click in my neck, and I felt a sharp, hot pain, and when he let go my neck it felt as if it was on fire, and it hurt to turn my head. I dropped to my knees gasping and crying, and then he left me, shutting the bedroom door behind him.

Everyone knew that he picked me up by my arm and dragged me to the room, but once inside I don't know if anyone had heard what he said, and if they did then no one said a word. After several minutes had passed I quietly opened the bedroom, my small frame trembling all over. I trembled so hard that I didn't think my legs were going to work. I lifted my bowed head, with a tear-stained face, and looked into the eyes of my mother. She was still seated with Lucy in her lap, and she gave me a small, sad smile. I forced my legs to move, and I ran out of the door nearest the room.

I didn't say anything to my mother or anyone else about what Derek had done. I was afraid to; if I did say something, he could get mad and do it again. I avoided everyone for the best part of the holiday after that. I was afraid to speak, afraid to smile, afraid to look at anyone, and I barely ate. I felt so distraught and confused inside.

Chapter Ten

Our little secret

My mother announced to me one morning "Your uncle Melvin is coming to stay wi us for a wee holiday."

Uncle Melvin wasn't really my uncle; he was of no relation to my mother at all. He was just a very close friend of Derek's. I had met him a few times before, but he never said much to me. Uncle Melvin was in his late fifty's or early sixties I think. He was tall, slightly round in the middle, with silver-white hair, a big nose, and wide thin mouth. When he came to visit he would always sit and drink with my mother and Derek, but he was the only one that drank this horrid smelling brown liquid, which was called brandy.

Later on the next day, a white car pulled up on the driveway. It was Uncle Melvin. I was given the task of taking his bags up into the back room, which was Lucy's nursery. Lucy's cot was placed in my room, and we were to share until Uncle Melvin went home.

I spent that day playing in the back garden, and then later in my room. All day long my mum, Uncle Melvin, and Derek were drinking and having a good time. Derek was more of a social drinker, not like my mother who drank every day. That evening my mum and Derek wanted to go to the British Legion club to listen to a band that was playing. Melvin offered to stay and babysit my sister and me.

That same evening I climbed up the cot and leaned down to give a sleeping Lucy a gentle soft kiss on her forehead. I then changed into my nightgown and climbed into my bed.

I roused in a sleepy state, to the sound of creaking. It sounded like it was from the last few top steps on the stairs. It must be my mum and Derek getting in from the club I thought, unconcerned, and so I snuggled deeper into the duvet and drifted back off to sleep.

I don't know how much time had passed from the creaking stairs when I was roused once again from my sleep. There was something tickling the top of my leg. I batted at whatever it was, and I felt my hand knock something solid, and warm. I quickly opened my eyes and sat bolt upright in my bed. My bedroom door was open about half way, and through the shaft of light that shone in from the upstairs hallway light, I saw the outline of someone sitting on the floor, about halfway along my bed. I stared, trying to make my eyes adjust to the darkness, frozen, in fear.

"Shh, it's me, your Uncle Melvin. I came to see you." His voice sounded deep, but soft as if to soothe me.

I could smell that horrible brandy that he liked so much.

"Don't you like me coming to see you? I thought we were friends." He drawled.

I didn't know what to say. I didn't want him to not be my friend, and so I said shyly: "I don't mind."

He came closer towards me, and I could see him a little more from the light in the open door. He was smiling at me. He stroked my hair and urged me to lie back down, and so I complied. Then his face got closer to mine, and he uttered: "can I kiss you goodnight?"

I nodded my head a little, and he pulled the duvet up to just under my chin and leaned in a little closer. I could feel his big nose brush against my little one. The smell of brandy was strong, and so I held my breath. His big wet lips covered my own much smaller ones. It seemed to last for forever and I released a whoosh of breath that I had been holding, and this made him draw back and laugh quietly.

"That felt good didn't it?" he asked me. seductively.

I felt uncomfortable, and I replied: "It was wet, and your breath is stinky."

He told me then, that that is how people kiss when the love each other. He was right, as that's how my mother and Derek kissed.

"This is our secret." He said "You mustn't tell Mummy or Derek or they won't let us be friends anymore. Tomorrow I will take you to the shops and buy you some sweets." He said Softly, But before he left he made me "promise not to tell anyone that he loved me", or "I would get into trouble."

I remember thinking Uncle Melvin was a strange man. He was different from Derek, he was much nicer. I wanted him to like me. I didn't want to be in trouble for not liking him or telling him not to kiss me anymore.

I agreed to keep the secret.

∞∞∞

The next morning, as I sat eating some cereal I caught Uncle Melvin looking at me. He put his finger to his lips when my mother wasn't looking. I nodded my head in agreement, and then I asked him aloud if he was taking me for some sweets?

My mum looked up and exclaimed "Evie! Don't be cheeky!. I'm so sorry about her Melvin"

"Uncle Melvin said he would take me to the shops," I stated flatly.

Uncle Melvin said, "It's okay I'll take her." And he winked at me, making me smile.

Over the next few days, Uncle Melvin pretty much ignored me whenever I came in from school. He smiled at me now and again, but didn't offer to take me to the sweet shop again, or come to kiss me goodnight, with his stinky breath and wet lips. Not until his last night, when he had offered to babysit my sister and me again.

∞∞∞

Little Lucy was once again fast asleep in her cot, and I was tucked up under my duvet unable to get to sleep. Every so often a train would go rumbling by, its wheels screeching as it prepared to stop at the station. I heard the familiar creaking sounds of the hallway stairs – someone was coming up.

Melvin peeked his head in around the door which was always left partially open. He then entered my room. I continued to lie in bed, as I assumed he was there to say goodnight – again.

"Are you awake?" he asked in a deep, slurry tone.

"Yes," I answered quietly.

Uncle Melvin walked over to my bed and sat down on the edge of it next to me. "I can't see you" he whispered, and he stroked my hair. "I've come to kiss you".

I lay unmoving, waiting, saying nothing, as he bent down and closed his lips over my own. I felt his warm, wet tongue pushing against my thin lips, trying to force them open. I turned my head away. I didn't like the feeling, his wet mouth, hot breath that smelled strongly of brandy.

"Shh, it's okay. I love you and that's how people kiss, and it will make you feel nice." He told me all I had to do was open my mouth and move my tongue.

"But I don't want to, it feels horrible," I said in a quiet, nervous protest.

"Let me show you that it's not horrible. It feels funny because you haven't done it before. I love you, let me show you." And he kissed me again, swirling his wet tongue around inside my mouth, trying to capture my own. I could feel his left hand touching my small thigh, his fingers felt warm and slightly rough, and then he found my most intimate part between my thighs. He began to fondle me; his breath was hot and heavy.

He began kissing me, and all the while I lay there frozen, confused. Nobody else did this to me I remember thinking. He sat up, continuing to fondle me, and he began doing something to himself in his lap. His breathing was shaky, and he was murmuring things to me about how pretty and soft I was.

After a little while, he stopped, pulled down my nightgown, covered me up, and told me not to tell anyone about what had happened, He said that it was "our little secret."

When he left my room I continued to lie there, unmoving, and unsure of what exactly I was feeling. I felt really sore between my legs where he had been rubbing me, and I felt itchy around my mouth and neck, where his scratchy silver stubble had been chaffing me.

I had to go to the toilet, but I was too scared to move. I thought that if he knew I was still awake then he would come back in my room and do it again.

I held it in till I just couldn't hold it in anymore. Warm pee seeped out, soaking my bed underneath my bottom. As I urinated it stung a little, and I felt painfully swollen. I eventually fell asleep, still lying in my urine soaked bed.

The next day Uncle Melvin left. He never looked at me or spoke to me, and I never told anyone about what he had done. I didn't want to get into trouble like he said I would. I was much too scared of Derek, and I knew my mother would not stop him if he hurt me.

Derek noticed when checking to make sure that my bed was made correctly, that had I had wet the bed, because I forgot to take the sheet off. Derek called me to my room, and called me a filthy animal for not using to toilet, and he cuffed me hard round the back of my head.

I cried as he stood watching me stripping my bed, and I must have got on his nerves with all my crying because he sent me off, muttering things about what I had done as I left the room.

Chapter Eleven

A bad egg

N early two more years had passed. My mother continued her drinking, and I barely saw her. I would
wake up, go to school, come home, play in my room
or outside, go to bed and repeat it all over again. I still went
to church on Sundays and the Vicar had encouraged me to join
the Brownies, and so I did, every Tuesday after school.

∞∞∞

Derek was still as mean as ever. He would sit at the head of the
dining table every evening and stare at me as I ate, picking at
the way I ate, which I didn't think was in any significant way,
compared to the way he noisily scoffed his food. But this one
particular evening he made me a boiled egg with toasted soldiers. As I began to eat it I realized it tasted disgusting. I gagged
and my eyes watered. I spat the egg out onto my hand.

"What's wrong with it?" he asked gruffly, still scoffing his own.

" It tastes nasty. I'm sorry Derek I can't."

"Get it bloody eaten you ungrateful tyke!" he shouted, whilst
glaring at me.

I looked down at the egg, it's clear, the slimy top now dripping
into the middle of it where I had scooped out my last teaspoon

full.

I picked up my spoon and dug out some thin, white egg, covered in the slime, and I put it in my mouth. Instantly I gagged again, my eyes watered, and the runny egg fell out of my mouth.

Derek slammed down the side of his fist on top of the dining table, making everything shudder.

"If you won't eat it then I will have to force it down you. Is that what you want?" he asked me angrily.

"No," I whispered quietly in response.

"Because you are not leaving this table unless you have eaten it!" he yelled.

I felt so tense and very scared, but I knew that if I swallowed the slimy egg then I was going to be sick. I picked up my small spoon once again, and this time my hand shook.

Derek got up abruptly and came striding round to the other end of the dining table, picked up my spoon and he tried ramming the egg into my mouth, scraping my teeth with the spoon, whilst berating me about how disgusting, and ungrateful I was.

My mother not really one for eating meals, as she was always happier with her larger's and snacking had heard the commotion and came through to the dining room.

"Derek, please," she said. "Don't make her eat it if she doesn't want it."

"Be quiet." He yelled at her. "When I tell her to eat she will fucking well eat it!" he yelled.

I saw my mother flinch a little.

I pushed my plate away, and it almost went crashing to the floor. That did it. He slapped me so hard that I felt my ears ring. My face stung and it hurt.

"Derek!" my mum called, holding onto his arm.

"She needs to be taught a fucking lesson!" He shouted, his eyes bulging with anger, and I actually thought that he would strike my mother.

Derek took me by the arm and dragged me up the stairs. I remember crying and shouting "Please stop, I'm sorry. I will eat it all up I promise."

I don't remember any verbal response, only the sharp feel of his thick leather belt buckle across my bare bottom cheeks. Thwack! Thwack! Thwack!

Oh, oh! the pain!, it hurt so bad I was screaming and screaming, and I didn't stop until after the third or fourth thwack of the belt on my small bottom. My mouth was open, tears were streaming down my face, but I could not scream, the only sound that came out was a high pitched squealing noise. He stopped for a moment only to begin using the leather part of the belt , and he hit me many more times.

Afterward, he left the room, and I sank to the floor on my knees. Oh my god, the pain was too much; it hurt so, so bad. I couldn't move. I just couldn't. I wanted the pain to go away so terribly, but it wouldn't.

My young bottom was covered in long red welts, and some of my skin was broken. I was unable to sit, lie down on it, even walking was agony.

My mother after a little while came upstairs, took me out of her's and Derek's bedroom and got me to lie on my side on my bed. My mother then gave me some sort of pink smelly cream, to put on my broken behind. My mother was so drunk by this time, and I couldn't talk for the pain.

For as long as I lived I knew no matter how many years went by, that I would never forget that night. It was one of the worst nights of my young life.

My mother did try speaking to me a little more after that incident, but she never tried to intervene between Derek and me again. I never understood why she wouldn't help me.

I remember it was only a few days later – because my bottom was still very sore when Derek called me to go and help him out the back garden, in his glass greenhouse. He wanted me to carry some plastic trays and fill them with soil. I was obedient, but remained quiet around him, as I helped.

Derek was trying to talk to me about what he was planting, but in my mind, I was hearing him, but not really listening, until he mentione'd that Uncle Melvin was coming for a visit, and he told me to make sure that I was nice to him. He said it as a mild sort of warning.

All I did was nod my head.

Uncle Melvin continued to visit, and each time he came into my room some nights when my mother and Derek were out. Uncle Melvin was becoming bolder with me, asking me to touch his erect manhood. I didn't ever want to, but I did. By this point in my life, I had learned to do what was asked of me without question, questions earned me a slap, or a kick, or worse – the belt.

Chapter Twelve

Help me

My mother was in the kitchen cooking, the smell of her homemade soup hung in the air. Lucy was having her afternoon nap, and Derek and Uncle Melvin were out.

"Mum?" I asked apprehensively.

"Yes, what is it?" She replied, with her back to me, busily stirring the pan of soup.

"Uncle Melvin keeps coming into my room when you are not here, and he's tickling me." I didn't know what it was he was doing, except that it was the only way to describe what his fingers were doing to my young body.

"Tickling you? What do you mean he's tickling you?" she asked now turned to face me with a confused frown.

I stared at her. I really didn't know how to describe it, and I felt afraid. I remained quiet and looked down at my feet.

"Don't be silly hen he's just playing with you."

"Okay. " I said. I really wished I hadn't said anything. I didn't understand what was happening to me when he came into my room. If my mother said it was Okay, then it must be, and so I walked away.

Chapter Thirteen

Answers

When I was eight years old, my mother sat me down at the dining room table and told me that my "real dad" was coming to see me. I never had any memories of my biological father, and I never once asked her about him either.

∞∞∞

My Dad's name was Peter, and I found out he was born in Canada and later raised in the United Kingdom.

I remember that when she told me about him that I didn't feel any sort of joyous excitement. I guess I was a little curious, and apprehensive at the same time. I also felt that he was someone else that I was supposed to get to know.

I accepted of course, and I went upstairs to go and pack some clothes in a small suitcase.

Looking back now I think he looked rather like a young Hugh Jackman, except he had a pale scar across his chin, which he got from a motorbike accident. We had the same curly hair, though he was light brown, and mine was almost white blonde. We had the same blue/green eyes and the same chin. He seemed nice, and he made me lightly giggle a few times at something funny he said or did. He talked a lot, about parts of the world he had seen, and I had never heard of before. He also got round to telling me how he had met my mother, and why he was never around before now.

Apparently, he had met my mother in a hotel in Blackpool. My father was a waiter, and my mother was a chambermaid. My mother had escaped an abusive home-life in Scotland, and my father was looking for opportunities elsewhere. Both of them liked to drink. My father's life was difficult. He was kidnapped by his father for many years; it almost broke my nan's (his mothers) heart. Then one day my father was dropped off on his mother's doorstep. I had no memory of ever meeting him, and I don't know whatever happened to him afterward. My grandfather was a bit of a rogue, and a drinker from what I was told. It wasn't long before he was dragging my dad around the pubs with him, and getting him drunk. When my dad returned to my nan he to was an alcoholic.

Nan never took a liking to my mum, but apparently, she was always very polite in her presence.

My parents got married rather quickly and they moved into a small flat in Worthing, West Sussex. In the month of September in 1979 my mother became pregnant with me. My Dad decided to become a DJ; it was good money at the time, and his business did really well.

When my mother discovered that she was pregnant my Dad bought for me a Paddington bear, and that is what he decided to call his DJ business. Paddington Bears Disco.

∞∞∞∞

I was born in the summer of 1980. My christening was held at the Thomas a Becket pub in West Worthing.

My parents' marriage eventually became quite strained with my dad working long hours, quite often away from my mother and I. My mother still continued her drinking, and my Dad had told me that she still continued to drink heavily, even through her pregnancy.

My Nan later told me that she had been trying to get in touch with my mother for almost two days so that she could come and see me. Apparently, My Nan had had enough and went round to the flat demanding to see me. Nan was shocked to find me in a cot with a heavily soiled nappy that hadn't been changed, in she didn't know how long, and the nappy had badly leaked, as I still continued to do my business. Apparently I had got terrible burns on my bottom from all the acid in my wee. Nan told me that She had me all cleaned up, and smothered my bottom in cream. I don't know what was said or done afterward with regards to that.

∞∞∞∞

It was around this time that my mother would keep taking or having me sent to Nanny and Pappys in Greenwich. London. My Dad said that he would get in from working late only to discover that I wasn't there, and he would have to drive all the way from Sussex to London to get me and bring me back home.

Dad, in the end, decided to move with us to Greenwich, London to be near Nanny and Pappy, hoping it would be easier for my mother if she had help with me. My dad got a job driving London, buses, and things were good for a little while.

∞∞∞

When I was two years old I became very ill, and I had developed some sort of fever. The Doctor according to my mother was very unsympathetic, and he told her that there wasn't much they could do for me if they couldn't get my temperature back down. My mother and nanna stayed up all night bathing me down and giving me medicine to help treat the fever.

My father had told my mother that he was going to be working late, and so she had tried contacting the bus depot to get them to deliver a message to inform him that I was very ill. The person that she was speaking to then had to tell her that they were very sorry but Peter was not, in fact, working that evening, and that he had not been scheduled to either.

My Dad came home the next morning and discovered that I was very ill. My mother was very distraught and threw him out – after he admitted to being with another woman. In her anger, she shredded all of his clothes, and threw them out into the street, and popped all four tires on his car.

After I had recovered from my illness my mother had decided to leave, and she went back to Sussex and she left me with my nanna and pappy on and off, for a few years.

Dad told me that Pappy was not actually my grandfather, he was nanna's boyfriend. My real grandfather she actually left after several years before because he was abusive, only for her to end up in another abusive relationship, with my Pappy. Nanna had decided to leave my pappy and She had to give me back to my mother, who was now living in a small flat in Worthing, West Sussex.

Nanna moved in with one of her eldest daughters in Scotland and passed away shortly before my half-sister Lucy was born.

Chapter Fourteen

Finding love

Before my father took me to his home in Kent, we stopped off at his mother's home. He told me that Nan was so looking forward to seeing me, because she hadn't seen me since I was a baby.

∞∞∞

We pulled up outside a beautiful big Tudor mansion; there were three or four floors. There was a large oak front door, and many windows with lead diamond shapes in the glass. Nan's house looked like something out of a children's storybook. There were green vines growing all over the front of the house, bright colored flowers in baskets, and smoke from two chimneys.

My father beeped the car horn, and after a few moments, the heavy oak door opened. Standing in the doorway was an elegantly dressed lady with deep burgundy wavy hair that was styled neatly framing her face. Nan's smile was huge; her green eyes were happy, and glassy, filled with tears not yet spilled. I smiled back, and Nan held her arms open and she embraced me soo fiercely.

"Hello, my darling," she said, "I have missed you."

∞∞∞

Nan was a scouse, born and raised in Liverpool. She married my grandfather who eventually became a drunk and a gambler. When he left her he took my father in spite. She once told me that in all the years that my father was gone, that she bought him a present every year for his birthday, and Christmas.

Nan had after several years met and married Alfred, a rich Banker, who bought her this wonderful home filled with expensive furnishings, and lavished on her wonderful gifts, and cruises all over the world. They adored one another, and Nan took such good care of him.

∞∞∞

Nan took my hand and we followed her into the study, which held a large fireplace. There was gold gilt-framed oil paintings, and china ornaments, and plates everywhere. I felt like I was sitting in the middle of a palace, and thought my Nan was a Queen! There was a door which led out into a wide and very long conservatory, and beyond the conservatory was a garden, bigger than I had ever seen, filled with bright colorful flowers, and trees as tall as a forest's. Nan caught me staring, and asked if I wanted to sit in the garden? to which I eagerly replied that I would love to.

Nan bought a silver tray, placing it on an iron patio set. On the tray were dainty cups and saucers trimmed in gold, a teapot and a plate filled with yummy biscuits.

I never discussed what my life was like, and she didn't ask me too many questions. I think she just wanted to find out for herself. Nan, my father and I spent the whole day sitting in her garden, talking and laughing. They let me wander the garden, with its many stone steps, bird houses, bird baths, and a big sundial. I even managed to find a little secret garden with a swing, hidden behind some bushes, and trees.

I was disappointed when it was time to leave, but before I left my nan handed me a fifty-pound note, kissed my cheek and promised that I would see more of her.

All I could do was stare at this red fifty-pound note I had never received money before, let alone fifty pounds. I was immediately thinking about all the things I could buy like sweets, a dolly for Lucy and flowers for my mum. Maybe I could buy something for Derek; I wasn't sure if I wanted to though. I thought if I did get him anything then it would be some handkerchiefs, as he always carried them, and was always blowing his nose.

Chapter Fifteen

Not alone

My father owned a large bungalow, with a long back garden that backed up into the woods. There were workshops and a swimming pool. Next to the bungalow was a white arctic lorry, with the words AZTEC Driver training on the side. The lorry was my father's, he was a very successful lorry driving instructor. I also found out the very next day that he was also a pilot, and he took me out in a four-seater plane from Biggin Hill airfield to Runcorn. He made me put on a pair of these big headphone's, and told me that they were like a telephone's and that we could hear and talk to one another - as the plane was so noisy!

I spent the whole week getting to know my dad. He showed me photographs of me as a baby and of himself with his lorry, as well as photos of nan and Alfred getting married. He put some of the photographs in an envelope for me to keep.

It was strange for me staying with my father, for one I wasn't used to being cooked meals, or given breakfast unless it was one of my mother's Sunday dinners. I was sent to bed each night at the same time, nine pm. It was also strange because although he drank like my mother, he was a lot more friendly and chatty. I wasn't used to being taken care of like this. I was too scared to tell him anything about my life in Sussex in case he told them, and I wouldn't be allowed to see him anymore. I already knew by now that no one liked a tattletale. I was just so happy to be there with him right there in that very moment, getting to know him and I didn't want anything to spoil it.

Chapter Sixteen

A fleeting happiness

D ad dropped me off, promising to see me again in the summer holidays. He handed me my case, a new purse with the money Nan had given me, and the envelope with the photographs. I kissed my dad on his presented check, and I stood on the driveway waving him off with a sad smile. I was going to miss him.

Inside my mum was sitting in the dining room with a glass of larger, Derek was laughing in the sitting room at some television programme, and Lucy was playing on the floor beside my mother. Out of everyone I had missed Lucy the most. I knelt down and gave her a cuddle. My mother told me to put my dirty clothes in the washing machine, and as I did she spied my new purse and envelope that I placed on the dining table.

"What's that you got?" she asked curiously.

"Dad bought the purse for me as my nan gave me fifty pounds!" I exclaimed happily.

"Oh did she? well give it to me, I'll take care of it for you." She said holding out her waiting hand.

I passed my mum the new purse, with the fifty-pound note inside, and I never saw the money that Nan had given me again.

Chapter Seventeen

Swim or sink

I felt hot and sticky. The very air I breathed in felt warm too. In the background, Whitney Huston's song "I wanna dance with somebody" was playing. I grabbed some of this small crunchy looking toast, called melba's and joined Derek at the hotel's breakfast table.

Outside was a little girl, about my age. She was in the blue sparkling swimming pool on a bright orange inflatable lilo bed, and she looked like she was having a great time.

∞∞∞

After breakfast, I went with my mum back to the hotel room, which was somewhere near the top floor, with a small balcony. We changed into our bathing suits and headed down to the pool with some towels.

Derek was really not one for sunning himself, but we found him laying on one of the sunbeds in a pair of shorts. My mother joined him, covering herself in Malibu tanning oil. I walked over to the pool where the little girl was still floating on her lilo.

"Hi," she said, grinning at me. "Are you getting in, it's a lot cooler in the water."

"I can't swim," I replied. The girl laughed at me, and then she saw how serious I was.

"I'll teach you, come on. Go to the other end its shallow; your feet will touch the floor."

"I won't drown will I?" I asked full of nerves.

"Nah you won't drown. I won't let ya, come on!" she called, as she waded through the water towards the shallow end, dragging her lilo behind her.

I sat down, dipping my feet into the lovely cool water. I watched as it rippled and shone, still feeling nervous.

The little girl urged me into the water, giving me her lilo to hold. She showed me how easy it was to swim by doing a length.

"What are you doing?" called Derek.

"I'm going to learn how to swim," I called back.

I heard some people laughing somewhere off to the side of me on the sunbeds. There were two older ladies watching me, and smiling. "Go on you can do it." One of them called out.

"There's only one way to learn," said Derek as he stood at the other end of the pool. "Come here." He beckoned.

"I'm okay," I replied, feeling safer where I knew my feet were now touching the bottom tiles of the pool like the little girl said. But when I told him"I'm okay" I could see it wasn't really a request – it was an order.

I gingerly got out of the water, and slowly made my way to where he was standing. The little girl followed me along from within the pool. The two ladies carried on chatting amongst themselves, and my mother was lying down on the sunbed, wearing sunglasses and covered in shiny oil.

"Come here ya scaredy cat" he taunted, with a smile. I had gotten within a couple of feet of him, when suddenly as quick as a flash he had grabbed me, throwing me outwards and into the air.

I remember screaming and hitting the water head first, and under I went with a scream. Big bubbles were coming out of my mouth, and they floated up past my face. I began kicking my arms and legs furiously, trying to reach for the surface of the water. I could see a blurry looking Derek, as he was still standing by the edge of the pool and leaning slightly over at me.

I was losing air, and I couldn't breathe. Just as I thought I was doomed a hand grabbed me and started pulling me up. When my head broke through the water I was gasping deeply for air. The little girl forced me to grab onto her bright orange lilo bed, and she started dragging it to the shallow end.

"Are you okay? Was that your dad?" she asked. I shook my head from side to side, still gasping.

I looked on and Derek was laughing, and he was saying something to my mother, but I didn't know what.

The two ladies were staring at me, and the one that told me before that "I could do it" was standing up halfway towards the pool and asked me if I was okay?

"I don't know " I responded, and then I said "yes". The lady looked so concerned. She looked at Derek who was now sitting back on his sunbed, and she shook her head at him.

I looked at my mum, but she was grabbing her handbag and towel, and then she left to go back into the hotel.

"That was horrible," said the little girl.

You would have thought that by Derek throwing me in, that

it would have put me off and sent me running for the safety of the hotel room. But I didn't. Instead, I stayed where I was, listening to the little girl's incessant chatter, which I didn't mind, I was grateful for it. I realized that if I never wanted that to happen to me again, and that I had better learn to swim, and swim well!.

By the end of the day, that little girl had taught me to swim on my back, kicking my legs, and then swimming forwards, by kicking my legs and putting my hands together to push away the water in front of me.

From the moment that I finally learned to swim, I didn't want to be out of that pool for the rest of the holiday. I don't remember that little girl's name, but even till this day I still thank her from the bottom of my heart. She saved my life that day and taught me how to swim.

Chapter Eighteen

My safe haven

I sat at the dining room table for what felt like hours, just waiting for my dad to pull up in his car. I was going to spend another week with him, and I was going to see my nan again. I was worried that she would ask me what I had spent the money on that she gave me, and I didn't want to lie and say that my mother had taken it. I decided that if she asked me I would just say that My mother was looking after it for me.

∞∞∞

As soon as I saw my Dad's little green spitfire with the top down rounding the corner I jumped up and ran towards the back door.

"Slow down you stupid idiot!." Derek called out. "Bloody pathetic" he mumbled.

I grabbed my suitcase and carried it slowly now to my waiting Dad.

"Aren't you going to put your buskins on?" Dad asked me. I looked at him in confusion.

"What are buskins?" I asked

"Buskins are shoes" he laughed.

I giggled to; it was a funny word for shoes. "I forgot them" I sighed.

"I will get them, you get in, and plug in your seatbelt love." He said, as he got out of the car and headed towards the house, and he was gone a few minutes before he returned, and he was frowning.

"Here are your shoes," he said handing them to me, and then getting in behind the steering wheel.

When we set off, he asked "if everything was okay with Derek and my mother? Because Derek was very rude when I said you forgot your shoes."

"Oh, he's always like that". I responded offhandedly. I just wanted to get to Nans and enjoy my time with dad, and Nan.

"I don't like him. He better be treating you right." Was all he said, and with that, we set off.

∞∞∞∞

That summer was the best I had ever had in my now nine years. Dad took me to the London zoo. It was the first time I had ever seen any sort of wild animal. I loved the orangutans; they were my favorite with their bright orange/red fur, small eyes, and bulging bellies. My dad did some very funny impressions of them. We ate burgers and enjoyed delicious ice-creams. At the end of our visit, he bought me a pencil case set with London zoo printed on it.

∞∞∞∞

Over the next few days, we visited MadamTussauds, wax museum, as well as the gates of Buckingham Palace, and we watched the changing of the guard. Dad bought some seeds so we could feed the pigeons – there were hundreds of them, and we rode through London on an open-top double-decker bus.

At night I would cuddle up in bed next to Robbie, a dog he had rescued from Battersea dog's home. Robbie was a shaggy, black, mixed deerhound. I had found my new best friend. Robbie would sneak into my room every night, and lie beside me in bed. My dad came in a few times to shoo him back out, but Robbie would come right back in again. Eventually, dad just gave up, and let Robbie and I snuggle together.

The day before he was due to take me back home, he decided to take me to a local riding school for my first ever horse riding lesson. I loved it! I told my dad that if ever got a horse when I was older I would name it Fiddy, after the pony that I had ridden. I was completely hooked on horses after that day.

Chapter Nineteen

Horse Fever

After spending that wonderful summer with my dad in Kent, I was once again back in West Sussex with my mother, Derek, and little Lucy.

∞∞∞

One day after school I decided to walk to the riding school, just up the road from my house. There were lots of beautiful horses, so big, and powerful, yet graceful. I thought that if I could help them take care of one, then they might let me ride, as I had no money, and mum wasn't really interested in getting me lessons.

I approached an elderly lady who was sitting in a little cabin surrounded by the scent of leather from the many saddles and bridles that took up almost all of the office space.

I don't know what this lady thought of a nine-year-old little girl asking quietly, barely louder than a whisper if I could do some work to ride a pony. She looked at me so puzzled and laughed.

"Have you ever ridden before?" she asked me.

"Y yes I have, once and his name was Fiddy," I answered a little nervously.

"Are you up here all by yourself?" she queried.

"Yes. My mum won't care, and I can't have the lessons, as it's too expensive she says." I could feel my mouth going dry. Maybe this was a bad idea. What if she told me to bugger off? Not that I wasn't used to being told that by now. I thought.

"How old are you?" she asked with a frown.

"I'm nine, almost ten," I responded quickly. The old lady stared at me for what felt like forever, and just when I thought she was going to send my skinny behind off packing, she didn't. Instead, she stood up and told me to go with her, and so I did. I followed her to a stable not too far away, and whatever was in there was kicking up such a fuss! I could hear banging against the door, loud whinnying, and snorting.

"This here is Henry; he is the same age as you funny enough, but I warn you he is a right grumpy bugger. See if you can calm him down."

My head was a little lower than the top of the stable door, and I got the fright of my life when this big brown and white cob's head popped out over the top of the door, still banging his foot against the lower one. I fell backward, feeling a heavy whoosh leaving my body as my rear end hit the dry dirt on the floor. I felt as if at any moment he was going to kick the stable door right down on top of me. I looked up at the lady, and she just nodded her head towards Henry.

"By the sounds of him, he doesn't have all day".

I didn't think so either. I thought in my head.

I stood up, brushing the dry dirt from my backside, and approached the door again, slowly. I looked into his big brown eyes, and I shakily put my hand up towards his face. As I did he opened his mouth and clamped his teeth down just inches away from my fingers. My heart started to hammer away like a hummingbird's wings deep in my chest.

"I'll be back soon, mind how you go." - Said the old lady.

What was the point in this? I thought. This horse didn't want to know me; he tried to take a chunk off me. I asked to help out with a pony, not this big brute! I didn't want to leave though.

"That wasn't very nice was it?" I admonished him. If you won't let me stroke you then I won't, I'll just talk to you."

I spotted a small tuft of grass poking out of the wall beside his stable, and so I yanked at it, pulling back with several straggly blades. I knew horses like to eat grass, Fiddy did.

Henry stopped kicking his door, and I held my shaky little hand up, ready to snatch it away if I saw his teeth again. He sniffed a little and blew out his nostrils with a snort. The grass flew off my hand. I tutted and grabbed the last of the grass sticking out. I breathed out heavily and held my hand out once more, and this time his muzzle made contact with the grass in my palm. I remembered being taught how to feed a horse properly when I was with Fiddy. You had to keep your hand really straight, as it was harder for them to catch you with their teeth. His muzzle brushed back and forwards over my palm scooping of the grass, which fell to the floor. I sighed. Ohh well at least he didn't bite me I thought.

The old lady appeared what seemed like out of nowhere and said "That's your first lesson, do not be afraid. If you are, then they can sense it. It makes them nervous."

"When can you start?" she smiled

"Right now." I grinned in response.

"Follow me." she beckoned. I thought I was going to see a pony, or maybe she would let me ride. Instead, she took me back into the office and told me to wait in a chair until she came back.

It was about ten minutes later when she came back with a younger girl. "This is my daughter Emma. Emma will teach you what you need to know, and then we will see about a pony."

I felt like my heart was going to burst with excitement and happiness.

Emma handed me some juice in a plastic cup, then pulled a book off of a shelf behind the desk.

"This is everything you need to know about horses, the different points of the body, what they are called. It also tells you how to groom them, and feed them."

I took the book eagerly.

Emma then gathered up some silver things caked in the grass and put them down in front of me.

"These are called bits, they go in the horse's mouth when you ride, and these help to steer the horse. They need a good clean, you can start with that. When you have finished let me know and then come and find me."

I cleaned those bits until they were all clean and shiny again. As promised I found Emma, not forgetting the book she gave me to read, and told her I was finished. Emma inspected my handiwork, and smiled, telling me I could come back the next day.

Over the next few weeks I returned every day after school, and from the moment I woke up on a Saturday, and Sunday I was there spending every waking moment that I could be around the horses and learning to muck out the stalls, what and how to feed them.

No one seemed bothered at home that I was spending less and less time there. I still wasn't free of Derek's temper and

I earned the brunt of it on many different occasions. Sometimes my young body hurt so much from the numerous slaps, and arm yanking that I struggled with some of the jobs at the stables, but it still didn't deter me.

I had been given a beautiful white pony to ride, and her name was Poppy. Poppy was Emma's pony when she was younger, and Emma felt that I was ready to start learning to ride. I was glad, not that I minded cleaning tack, or mucking out the stables, or even carrying buckets upon buckets of heavy water, not if it meant that I had Poppy!

∞∞∞

I struggled to find the trotting rhythm during lessons, so the next day after school, before going to the stables, I flung across the high garden fence, my brown parker jacket. I managed to climb up onto the other end of the fence and shimmied my way along to my jacket. I sat on top of it, and put my feet into the coat pockets as if they were stirrups, and my jacket was the saddle. I took my skipping rope out of my waistband, and flung it over the fence post – they were my reins, and the post was the pony's head.

I imagined Poppy going into a trot, and so I pushed down with my feet to stand a little – pretending it was a rising trot. Up and down I went, learning to keep my balance, and finding a rhythm. I was so into it that I didn't notice the fence getting really wobbly, or that the pockets on my parker were ripping until it was too late!

I fell sideways whilst still atop the garden fence. I quickly scrambled myself up and ran. I ran all the way to the stables without stopping. I was so scared about how much trouble I would be in, not only had I broken the fence. I had ruined my jacket. I did the first thing that I thought and that was to see

Emma.

By the time I got there I was crying, soo afraid. I had never told Emma or her mother about Derek, my mother or Melvin, but I did often talk about my dad and Nan. For the first time ever Emma took me into her family home, and she made me cheese on toast.

I think Emma and her mum had sensed something was not right, maybe because I was always there, I never spoke of being at home, and today I was so blatantly afraid. I had always taken myself back home on foot, but that evening she took me home by horse and trap. It was the first time I had ever been on one. It was way better than being in a car. I thought, and when I was old enough I would get myself a horse and cart and travel everywhere in it.

Emma stayed until I had gone into the house and closed the door. My mother came to me quickly and told me to go to my room. Nothing happened to me that night I don't know why. I think maybe my mother had something to do with it.

The next morning my pockets on my jacket were fixed.

Thank you, mum. I love you. I thought that night, as I fell into a deep exhausted sleep.

Chapter Twenty

Sex education

The classroom was buzzing with giggles from my classmates. Our teacher was putting images onto the projector, displaying scientific images of a male and female's genitalia onto the big whiteboard at the front of the classroom.

I looked around at the row of boys to my right, they were whispering and sniggering to one another, but I could hear that they were talking about a girl in front of them. There were three girls sat to my left, and they were laughing and pointing at the image of the male's genitals. I remember thinking why is it so funny? Had they not seen a real one, like me?

"It's gross isn't it?" the girl beside me asked.

"Have you seen a real one?" I asked her. The girl looked at me with a disgusted face

"Eww, no way!" she said. "My mum says you're not supposed to, not until you are like way older."

I felt my face grow hot, and it only seemed to get hotter by the minute. Was I the only one that had ever seen and touched a real one? Something just didn't feel right... at all.

The teacher hushed the classroom, as it was getting noisier by the second. It was time for us to listen to her explain about the male, and female bodies, how they worked, and all about puberty.

I was lucky enough at 11 years old, to have not gotten my period yet. I didn't even really have breasts, not like several of the other girls in the classroom. I was glad, as a lot of the boys in class would tease those girls, and make funny gestures on their own chests.

The final talk that the teacher gave was about privacy and prevention of pregnancy. The teacher explained that it was very important, especially at our ages to dress and undress in private, and she continued to explain that now we were in middle school and at very important developmental stages in our lives, that this is why we are now given separate changing rooms with lockable doors.

Then the teacher after going through conception, and pregnancy, went on to give a firm speech about how a sexual activity should not occur until we were sixteen, or older. We should not feel under any pressure before this age, not only was it illegal, it was also unsafe, as our bodies were still in a state of development.

I felt sick, the room felt like it was tipping from side to side, and I was trembling.

"Miss! there's something wrong with Evie!" some girl called out. I don't know who. I could not focus.

I don't remember being taken from the classroom, or anyone speaking to me. I don't even know how I came to be sitting in the school nurse's room, but now there were two teachers, an old school nurse, as well as the principal. They were all gathered around me, calling my name, and staring at me.

The school nurse knelt down in front of me; taking my hand within her warm wrinkly one.

"Evie, what's wrong sweetheart? Come on you can tell me, its okay." She soothed.

I felt too ashamed inside. I was a bad girl. I did things that I wasn't supposed to, and so did Uncle Melvin! Oh my god, no, no, no! My mind was screaming. Everyone is going to hate me, hate me, hate me!

"It has something to do with my lesson I'm sure. She's just not like this. I've never seen her act like this." I heard my teacher saying.

"Please" urged my teacher, as she too now was knelt beside the nurse, and resting her hand upon my shoulder. "What is it Evie, are you unwell?"

I shook my head from side to side.

"Maybe," the nurse said "Evie would feel better if it was just her teacher and I, maybe you will tell us Evie?" she asked encouragingly.

The other teacher, whom I didn't really know, agreed to leave the room along with the principal. I didn't respond. I could only stare vacantly at the clock on the wall across the room. It read 2:45 pm.

"I can't go home," I said quietly, and I know I must have looked completely deadpan.

"What do you mean you can't go home darling?" asked my teacher.

I couldn't answer her. I could not speak, as I felt this hot ball of fire burning in my throat, as I desperately tried to hold back my sobs. All I could think was oh my god, oh my god!

The nurse stood up, as well as my teacher and the teacher said "Evie I will be back in a moment okay. I'm going to get you a nice glass of juice."

I didn't acknowledge her at all I just continued to stare at the clock, but now I was rocking my small body back and forth, back and forth, on the hard plastic chair I was sitting on.

"Evie has someone done anything bad to you?" asked the nurse once the teacher had left, closing the door.

I looked at the nurse, her soft white hair all done up in a loose bun, her thin glasses were perched on the end of her nose, and her lips were thin and pressed firmly together.

"Please, please don't tell my mum or Derek, please!" I begged, and I began relentlessly sobbing.

"Go on. I promise I won't tell anyone, but you must tell me, dear." She urged, and this time she took another chair and placed it in front of me, and sat down.

It seemed like a long time before I could speak. I was torn between telling the nurse or not telling her. I was going to be in so much trouble if I did. I continued to cry. I cried for all the memories of Melvin visiting me in my room. I cried for every lash of Derek's belt hitting my young body that time when I couldn't eat the egg. I cried for every mean thing that was ever said to me at home, and then I cried… in anger!

I began to feel a hot rage building up inside of me. I wanted to smash and break everything in the room, but I didn't. Instead, I began to rock myself harder and harder. My breathing became rapidly loud in my ears. I couldn't focus. My young mind was in such a whirl, it was like my brain was spinning, and spinning.

"You need to calm down Evie please, you must keep calm." urged the nurse.

My teacher re-entered the room, and she tried handing me a plastic beaker with juice, but I couldn't take it.

"Come on Evie, it will help. Take this drink for me, and let me get you a paper towel for your face. Your pretty face is all blotchy."

I heard the sink running in the corner of the room, and then the teacher was blotting my swollen face with a cold, wet paper towel. Afterward, she took the beaker from my hand

and put it up to my lips to drink. Mechanically I drank, and I didn't acknowledge the wet paper towel on my face.

"Evie was about to tell me what was wrong, but only if I promised not to tell anyone, so I promised." The nurse said to the teacher.

"Okay," the teacher responded slowly. "Do you mind if I stay Evie? To be honest, it's quieter in here than my noisy classroom, and I would rather sit here with you… for a little while – if that's okay?" she finished quickly.

I shrugged my shoulders and looked down at my hands, which were clasped so tightly together and now looked a shade of white and blue.

"M my uncle he made me do bad things to him," I said it so quietly, barely above a whisper. I heard a whoosh of breath from my teacher, and the nurse stood up. I began sobbing again, and I felt like my insides were turning inside my chest as I cried. My chest began to almost ache as I cried great gut-wrenching sobs.

"Evie. I need to check on my class, but I will be right back I promise." And again I was left with the nurse, who put her arms around me, and she said "it will all be okay now, it will all be okay. Just let it all out. The nurse drew back, but she continued to rub my back in small circles until my teacher returned.

Chapter Twenty One

I'm falling

I was riding in the back of a police car, being taken to Worthing police station. I don't remember the journey, and I don't remember what I told them, but I did tell them everything that had happened at home and with Uncle Melvin. I was still too afraid to tell them about Derek, and how angry he was going to be.

∞∞∞

Next, it was dark, and I was sitting in the back of a lady's car. I can't remember anymore what she looked like, but she told me that she was a social worker and that she was on her way to my house to collect my things.

"Collect my things? Why? Can't I just go home? I'm tired now." I said.

"It is complicated Evie. Your stepfather doesn't want you to return, and your mother is standing by him I'm afraid. They want you to stay in the car whilst I wait at the door for your suitcase."

"Why? I want to see my mummy. I don't want to leave, where am I going? Is my daddy coming to get me? Why don't they want me? I'm sorry! I didn't mean to do anything wrong. I'm sorry!" I cried, begged and pleaded.

But the social worker just looked at me sadly. We can't get a hold of your father. Your mother doesn't want you with him, she would rather you stay with foster parents Evie, I'm sorry."

"Foster parents?" I asked, sobbing.

"Yes, we have families that look after children when they have no families or any other place to go. You will be okay Evie, The foster parents you are going to are very nice. They have a nice big house, and garden, as well as two other children. They will take good care of you."

But I didn't know this family! They don't know me. What about my mummy, when can I see my mummy?."

"I don't know yet Evie. We have a lot to sort out, but we will. We are driving to your new home tonight. You can have a sleep in the car I'll ask your parents for your pillow and bed covers okay?"

When we pulled up outside the familiar sight of home, all I wanted to do was get out of the car, and run into the house, and into my room. I didn't want to leave them no matter how bad it was. I didn't want to leave Lucy or the stables. I would never see Emma, her mum, or Poppy again. What have I done!

Chapter Twenty Two

Devil the goat you know

I had been living with my foster parents for about three weeks. They were okay. I missed my mother, Lucy, and the stables more than anything. I would cry every night before I went to sleep, and I would cry again when I woke up. I cried till there were no tears left to cry, and then I developed a slight moaning tick.

∞∞∞

One day I was playing out the back in a small field of grass, and Their grumpy old billy goat had chased me halfway across the field until I reached the safety of the large wooden climbing frame. I was stuck there until someone came to get me, or the raggy goat got sick of waiting to sink its crooked teeth into me.

I had been sitting up on the climbing frame for a good hour, with the goat's beady eye fixed firmly on me the entire time, when my foster mother called out my name.

"Your mother is on the phone, come quickly!"

My mum! Damn that goat. I took off one of my shoes and threw them in the opposite direction. The goat took after my shoe, and I ran clear across the grass without looking back at the demon goat. All I was thinking as I ran was my mother! She's on the phone!

My mother was supposed to call me once a week, but up until now, she hadn't, and I was so happy! now that she was finally calling me.

∞∞∞

It was wonderful to hear the sound of her voice, though I felt really sad and incredibly homesick too. I told her how much I loved and missed her, and Lucy, and I must have said sorry I don't know how many times. I didn't feel particularly close to my mother really up until this point in my life. My mother was familiar. My Mother was my connection to everything I knew and missed.

"when can I come home?" I asked with hope in my voice.

My mother was quiet for a little bit, before telling me that "she didn't know."

I asked her desperately if anyone had managed to get in touch with my dad?"

"Why? Aren't you happy there?" She asked a little sulkily.

"If you don't want me, then I would rather stay with Dad than live here. He loves me, I know he would want me to live with him, I know it." I said trying to hold back my sobs.

The telephone line clicked, and the line went dead. "Mum, mum, are you there? Mum?" She was gone.

She must have hung up the phone. I ran back out of the house, towards the climbing frame again. I didn't see the goat; my foster mum must have put him away. When I got to the top I sat on the flat roof of the climbing frame once more, and I cried as if my heart was breaking into a million pieces. I heard my foster mum call out my name, but I didn't look up at the house.

Chapter Twenty Three

Going home

I don't know how long I sat there, but the sun had started to go down. I heard my name being called again.

I climbed down, and slowly made my way back to the house.

"Your mum is on the phone." called my foster mum.

I wasn't as elated this time, but I still wanted to hear her voice. I picked up the telephone, and said "Hello."

"Evie, its mum. You're coming back home to live. Derek and I have talked about it, and he's agreed."

I wasn't sure if I heard her right. "What about Melvin? Will I still see him?" I asked timidly.

"No, he's not allowed to come to the house anymore." She said firmly.

"Why are you letting me come home?" I asked warily.

"Because you are my daughter, and you belong with me. I don't want you to chose your dad over me, it upset me. Now pack your thing's because tomorrow you're coming home kid!" she said elatedly.

I don't remember the journey back home to West Sussex, and I don't even remember my first day back.

I never saw another social worker again, and after a few weeks,

I settled back into my old routine of getting myself up for school, getting breakfast, making my packed lunch. When I got home at the end of the school day I was back at the stables with Emma and her mum. They were curious as to where I had been but didn't probe. In the evenings I would make myself something to eat, using the fat fryer.

∞∞∞

My dad had been working abroad for a couple of months. He had no idea what had happened to me until he returned and listened to the answerphone message that the police and social worker had left him. When I next saw my dad he had come down by train, as he had just lost his license for three years, and had to pay a hefty fine for driving under the influence of alcohol.

Dad took me back with him by train to stay for another week. During my visit, he asked me several light questions about what Melvin had done. I didn't call him Uncle Melvin anymore, for one he wasn't my real uncle and two because I despised him.

Dad was really upset, and made several verbal threats like "just wait till I get my hands on him." And "I'll find out exactly where he lives."

I never said anything in response, but my Dad had told me that Melvin had been questioned by the police, but he didn't know anything other than that. I tried my very best to forget about what he had done, but it was very difficult.

∞∞∞

In the first few days and months since I was taken away, I had taken to bathing and washing a lot at very random times. I would scrub my body using a nail brush covered in soap, two and sometimes three times a day. I made my skin burn and bleed with all the scrubbing. All I wanted was to wash Melvin off my body. It didn't matter how much I scrubbed. I would close my eyes, see him and feel like I needed to scrub my already sore body again over and over.

I was glad he wasn't allowed to come to the house anymore, more so because during his last few visits I had caught him watching little Lucy who was only five years old. I watched his eyes following her. I saw the way that he looked at her when he picked her up and put her on his knee, it was the same way he looked at me when he was going to touch me.

The last time he visited me in my room he asked me if I thought Lucy could keep a secret If he were to love her as well?

I said no. and told him that she couldn't. At the time still not knowing if what was happening was right or wrong I was afraid, and I didn't want him to share secrets with Lucy. If I didn't like it, then neither would Lucy.

Knowing afterward that what Melvin had done to me was wrong, I was glad that it came out, and I was so relieved because now Lucy was safe, and she wasn't living what I was going through. I felt that I had saved not only myself but little Lucy too. I loved Lucy, she was the only one who didn't treat me like I didn't belong or exist. I loved her cute little smiles and giggles. When I was sad or lonely, she would run and put her little arms around my neck and hug me.

Chapter Twenty Four

Calm before the storm

Derek had spent my first few months back saying very little to me, which was of course unusual. I think now it was because he was unnerved because I had told the social workers and police about his best friend Melvin, I often wondered if he was also nervous that maybe I would speak up about him too. I would n't have, because I didn't want to go back to foster care. I would rather have lived through anything he gave me than to go back into care.

Like any predator though, they wait for their moment to strike.

I had come home from the stables one evening. Mum was out at my aunties, and Derek had locked the back door. So, I went round to the front and rang the bell.

"Who is it?" he called out.

"It's Evie! the back doors locked."

"For fuck's sake!" he shouted and went to the back door to unlock it.

I forgot the cardinal rule! - To take my boots off before I came inside.

"Take your fucking shoes off, before you come in this house! You imbecile."

I felt myself cowering. I started to make my way back outside, to take off my boots when he grabbed a hold of my hair. I felt searing hot pain, as he pulled.

"Look! Look at the state of this fucking floor that your mother just cleaned!" he roared down into my face. His nose was almost touching mine. "You can bloody well clean it, go on!" he shoved my head forwards down onto the kitchen floor and was rubbing my face into the dirt from my boots.

"Get up" he spat breathlessly. "Come on, get this shit cleaned up."

I tried getting to my knees, there was spit hanging from my mouth, and when I finally managed to painfully stand in a hunched position he was glaring at me.

"Look at you. You're fucking disgusting. Don't stand there like a gormless twit. Get the mop and bucket.

I took off my boots and put them in the understairs cupboard, where all the coats and shoes were, along with the mop and bucket.

When I came back Derek was sitting at the dining table, looking at a newspaper, and blowing his nose. I tried to move about as quietly as possible, but also as quickly as I could, so that I could go up to my room.

"You should never have been born," he said darkly and without looking at me.

I wasn't crying, but I began taking sharp ragged breaths in as if I was. Every time that I breathed in, my throat would get sucked in.

"Nobody wants you." He said.

"T that's n not, t true, my d dad w wants me He loves me."

83

I couldn't get my words out for stuttering and for my breath that kept getting sucked in.

"Your dad's a fucking idiot, just like you."

"I I'm g gonna t tell m my m mum."

"Tell you bloody mother I don't care and neither does she! All the trouble you have caused. It serves you bloody right, You're an animal."

I ran right out the back door, with no shoes. I ended up on Lancing beach crying, and incessantly talking to myself over, and over.

I hate him! I hate him! I yelled at the crashing waves. Please, someone, come and take me away! Please… please… please. HELP ME. I don't want to live anymore.

I thought about going into the sea and letting it take my young body. I thought about running in front of a car on a busy road and getting sucked beneath its wheels.

Chapter Twenty Five

Emptiness

When I got home after spending the night huddled inside the small porch of a beach hut, my suitcase, and several black bags were waiting for me.

"Your uncle Joseph (my mum's brother) is taking you to Greenwich, to live with your pappy and his new wife Mary."

"Mum noo p please!"

"I don't want to hear it. You're going and that's

∞∞∞

I never got a chance to tell my mum what Derek had done and said the night before, but I knew that it was Derek's doing. I think that he told her that me being back at home was not working and that it was better if I wasn't living there, or some such thing.

I don't know why she didn't call social services to put me back into foster care, and with a Pappy that I barely remembered, except for his singing, dancing and giving me suckie dummies. I hung my head and waited for my uncle Joseph to take me away.

∞∞∞

Pappy seemed to me as rather cold and aloof, and nothing like I once remembered. His wife Mary made more effort by taking me to Catford market to get me kitted out for my new school. Mary also bought me a fur coat with a matching muffle, and a pair of pink silk pajamas, but I couldn't return her enthusiasm or her smile. I just didn't care.

After a week or so, they gave up trying to get me to talk, or smile and they barely spoke to me at all. They fed me, clothed me and gave me money for my bus fare to Thomas Tallis School.

One day though one of the boys at school teased me, and I ran away. I got on the bus back to Pappy and Mary's.

I explained to pappy what had happened, and he looked as if he felt a little sad for me. He made as if to put his arms around me, but stopped. Pappy walked away from me saying. "I Can't." he dropped his arms and walked away from me.

Looking back now I think that he was afraid, that maybe I would say he had done something to me. I was someone to be afraid of, and I was a stigma.

A few days later he took me to his favorite pub - Tonky's bar. Pappy was a drinker just like my mother, and my dad, so I was used to the slurred speech and defiant talks when they got angry over something. Pappy began yelling about Melvin, calling him all kinds of defamatory names.

"How could he? HOW COULD HE DO THAT TO YOU!" he yelled. Everyone in the bar turned and looked at Pappy and me.

"H he's spoiled you!" he slurred.

"I'm not spoiled Pappy," I whispered.

"What do ye mean? Of course, you were unless you were lying?"

"No Pappy I was telling the truth. I'm not spoiled though. I'm not bad."

"Get te fuck! Go home." He shouted.

So I ran. I ran to the Thames River near Pappy's house, and I went through the long tunnel to the canary wharf on the other side of the river. I sat on a bench huddled up and watched as longboats went backward and forwards. I didn't stay long. It was freezing. I made my way back through the tunnel, to the other side. I passed the black cannons, the cutty sark ship, and knocked on the front door. Mary answered.

"What time do you call this?" She shouted.

I was sick of shouting. I was sick of being shouted at! And so I told her exactly that.

Pappy was sitting in his rocking chair. The smell of Guinness was potent.

"William are you gonna let her speak to me like that?" she shrilled at him, but glaring at me.

"Stop being a BITCH!" I screamed.

Pappy strode over to me and grabbed me by the throat, and gave me a sharp stinging slap.

"Apologise to Mary. You don't talk to her like that after every-thing she's done for you!" he shouted, and then released me.

"Sorry Mary". I said looking at her shocked face, for I don't think she expected Pappy's reaction towards me.

"Get to bed" hen she said kindly, nodding her head towards the door.

∞∞∞

I have always felt bad for yelling at Mary like that, and calling her a bitch. Mary was actually a very sweet woman.

Chapter Twenty-Six

Running

I lay in bed fully clothed in the dark bedroom, waiting. As soon as I heard Mary and Pappy going to bed, and closing their door I got up. I grabbed my coat and a backpack that I had stuffed with some clothes. I then put my shoes on and made my way over to the window. I lifted it up and climbed out.

I walked through Greenwich center and carried on past the Queens House museum. A car pulled up beside me it was a young man." Are you okay?" he asked. But I didn't answer him. I kept on walking until I ended up at the Elephant and Castle.

∞∞∞

Several well wrapped up; raggy looking people were huddled up on the floor, of a tunnel. They were each pressed tightly against the white tiled wall. A young woman with long black dreadlock hair and a lip piercing was asking passers-by for some spare change. She didn't look very well, and she kept coughing. A little further down was a man about the same age as her. His hair was a messy brown, and his clothes looked dirty and mismatched. I listened as he played a fast tune on a recorder. I remember thinking that he was very good. I had learned to play Frère Jacques at school on the recorder, but that was about it.

I decided to sit down and listen to him play. I was feeling so sleepy, and my feet were sore from all the walking. I woke up to the sound of a chink! A lady had passed me and thrown some money down in front of my crossed legs. I wanted to tell the lady that she had dropped some money, but then I saw a man throwing money down to the lady, and he carried on walking. I quickly realized that we were being given money... for sitting in the tunnel. Over the course of the night several more passers-by had thrown money down to me, and in the early morning rush hour, I was thrown yet more money from people quickly bustling in and out of the tunnel on their way to work. By the time I stood up I had almost twenty pounds.

The young woman with the long black dreadlocked hair and lip piercing came over and sat down beside me. "You're a little bit young to be out here on the streets." She said.

I didn't know how to respond, so I just nodded.

"You did alright for yourself. Better than us lot in here." she smiled. "It's because your young, and they feel sorry for you, but not sorry enough to help you." She frowned.

"I don't want to go back to my Pappy's. I want to go back home, but it's too far away." I said sheepishly.

"Well if you're not happy, then you shouldn't go back. Bad was it?" she asked with a frown. I just nodded.

"I am staying in a hostel tonight, but it will be full. It's not safe for you to sleep out here. There are too many bad people about. If you like I can ask my friend if you can stay with him, he will look after you, until you decide what you want to do."

"O okay," I replied. I wasn't sure I liked the sound of it, but if it was her friend then maybe it was okay.

"I'm Nastazia by the way. My friend is Dilk; he's right down there, the one playing the recorder."

I gave her a small smile, as she walked away. What funny names I remember thinking. Nastasia returned with Dilk about five minutes later.

"Hey." Dilk grinned. "I hear you need a safe place to stay. Where are your people? The ones that you want to get to?"

He didn't sound like he was from England, but his English seemed pretty good. "In Sussex, well Lancing." I stood up, playing with the change in my almost full pockets.

"What is your name little one?" he asked me.

"Evie," I told him, though I wasn't sure If I should have told him my name. Well I thought, it's a bit late now!.

"Well, I am safe. I won't let anything happen to you. I don't have much, but I will share it with you, and teach you some things. But if I was you, I would use your money to get back to your people. Being homeless is not safe, especially for one so young. How old are you?" He asked.

"I'm eleven and a half," I responded quietly.

"Jesus," Dilk muttered. "This is much too young. Are you running to be safe?" he asked me with sadness.

"Yes, well sort of. I don't know who wants me. But I'm going to try and get back to my mum… if I can."

"Well get your bag and follow Me." he then turned and said some words to Nastasia. Nastasia smiled at me and gave me a small wave. "I will see you again soon."

Chapter Twenty Seven

Chequers and content

I spent about a week with Dilk, in an old rundown townhouse. Some of the windows had the glass missing, and the walls inside were now just bare brick, like the outside. There was however a badly charred fireplace and Dilk soon had us warmed up in no time, burning paper and wood. The flooring had badly rotted planks of wood, and we had to be careful where we stepped.

Dilk gave up his usual bed; a dirty mattress, littered with several blankets, and no pillow. He taught me how to keep warm by stuffing any sort of paper we could find under our clothes. I crinkled like a crisp packet when I moved, but I was surprisingly very warm.

A little later on Dilk left me, to buy some food with the money I had collected from my first night. When he returned, he handed me a sandwich, and a bottle of fizzy pop. I looked to see what he had bought for himself, but I couldn't see anything else in his hands. I asked him why not, but he said that he refused to buy himself anything with it because it was my money, and I had earned it fair and square.

"Come with me." He said, "There is something I want to show you."

I followed him without hesitation, down the rickety, falling apart staircase, and out of the house. We walked for about five minutes or so until we came upon some large wheelie bins behind a food store. I could smell fresh bread from somewhere very close by, and it made my mouth water... I was thinking about the ham sandwich that I still clutched in my cold hand.

Dilk looked around him cautiously before sliding back the bin lid and peering in. I couldn't see what was inside as it much higher than me. He let out several breathy grunts, before pulling free whatever it was that he held.

"What is it?" I asked cautiously, at the bundle of lettuce, and something in a brown paper wrapping.

"This." He said is where I eat. Dilk smiled, looking rather pleased with himself at his find.

"They throw out some really good food, and it's still sort of fresh. It doesn't hurt you. Do you want some?"

I remember standing there thinking that it sounded, and looked completely disgusting! But I tried not letting it show on my face. He looked so happy, and I didn't want to offend him in any way.

"You don't need to buy anything when you can get it for free. You will need to learn this if you plan on living rough. I didn't make enough last night, and so this is where I come.

"Living rough?"

"Yes. When you don't have anywhere to live, it means that you're homeless. People treat you like the dirt underneath their fingernails, or they will try to avoid you altogether. You need to be smart, and learn how to survive. You can't always rely on strangers giving you money, or busking or whatever.

"Busking?" I asked rather confused, and he laughed at me a little.

"Busking is when you have a talent of some sort and use it to make money. I'm a mere busker because I play my pipe, that's how I get money. Others with little tools or talent, well they are beggars... they beg for money.

"Ohh... so I was begging?" I asked after gaining a little under-standing.

"No. Actually, you were neither. You're just a kid, and well they feel sorrier for you. All you had to do was sit there". He stated rather flatly. "People probably assumed that you had no parents, or that they were sitting elsewhere begging."

"Right," I responded slowly as if I was gradually beginning to understand. "Though I wasn't busking, begging... or whatever. I just sat down to rest, and listen to you playing your pipe. I noticed he didn't call it a recorder, and so I said pipe. "You're good though, better than me. I only know one tune." I said smiling.

We headed back to the run-down house. The fire had all but burned out in the fireplace. Dilk threw on some more wood, and afterward, we both settled down, me with my shop bought a sandwich, and Dilk who managed to make a meal out of his bin finds.

∞∞∞

Before I slept that night he taught me how to play chequers, a game similar to chess, but less complicated for me to under-stand at that time. I enjoyed it, and so did Dilk. I actually thought that maybe he was just really grateful for the com-pany too.

Chapter Twenty Eight

Going home

It had been over a month, and Dilk and I had managed to get to know each other pretty well. He had never asked me what had happened to make me run away from my Pappy's, but he didn't try and get me to go back either. I was scared in the first few days, thinking that he would go to the authorities, and tell them about me, but again he didn't.

Dilk went out a few times, telling me to stay in the house where it was safer, and every time he bought me food from the shop. I think he guessed that I wasn't impressed with eating leftover food from the bins, despite me never saying anything.

∞∞∞

One morning though I woke up and was feeling fed up, and so I decided to sit with him and listen to his music. Dilk didn't seem to mind that, for he said I brought him good luck, and people always threw him more change.

When I got to the tube station tunnel he wasn't there, and so I sat in his usual spot. The tunnel was packed full of people in expensive looking clothes, rushing always rushing. I started to feel a little uncomfortable when a large man wearing a long black coat and a black detective looking hat kept walking by me. He was tall and slightly well rounded, maybe in his forties.

I remembered what Dilk had told me about evading when I felt that I was being followed or in danger. I don't know what this man was doing, but it definitely felt as if he was stalking me. As he passed me for about the fourth time I quickly got up, and I ran. I ran the only way I could, which was in the same direction as the large man. When I had gone past him I didn't stop until I was outside the entrance to the Elephant and Castle shopping center. I stood trying to catch my ragged breath, glad that I had gotten away from the tunnel, and out in the open amongst the throng of the crowd. As I looked around I spotted him, at the same time he spotted me, and he began heading in my direction. I turned around, running straight into the shopping center and up a flight of stairs.

I found a good hiding spot behind a large advertising banner in the upper floor window. I took my backpack off my shoulders and sat down. Every now and then I peered around the banner, and to my surprise after several minutes, there was the man. He was standing about a hundred yards away, looking all around I was sure... for me. He looked frustrated.

I stayed where I was for about two hours or more before I felt that it was safe enough to leave. It wasn't until I had reached the ground floor that I remembered my backpack! I had left it on a bench next to the banner, whilst I put my coat back on.

I quickly took the stairs two at a time. By the time I had gotten to the top in view of where I had left my bag, there was security and several police officers.

Ohh no! They were looking for me, and one of the policemen had stopped someone from going towards my backpack. They were treating it as if it was something dangerous. I was annoyed, all I wanted was my bag back, but it wasn't worth it to get caught, and taken back to Pappy's.

I made my way back to the house, and Dilk was pacing the floor.

"Where have you been? I've been looking all over for you!" he exclaimed.

I managed to explain to him that a big man had been following me and that when I had lost him, he then tried looking for me.

"I'm glad you okay because I got you something." He said smiling

"You have? Okay?"

Dilk presented me with a long strip of paper. "What is it?"

"That is your ticket home. It doesn't go to Lancing, but it does go to Worthing, and I'm sure that you can make your way from there."

I couldn't believe it! Dilk had bought me a national express one-way ticket... to home.

"H how did you get it Dilk?" I asked with tears streaming down my face.

"I busked for it and saved the money. When I had enough I went to the coach station and got the ticket."

So that's where he was earlier when I couldn't find him, he was at the coach station.

"Thank you Dilk. I whispered smiling through my tears.

"You're welcome." He replied, looking a bit bashful.

The next morning Dilk took me to the bus station to board the coach bound for Worthing.

"I'm going to miss you Dilk."

"I'm going to miss you too little one. Make sure you go straight to your mum's and try and sort things out." He said ruffling my head.

"Thank you for looking after me. I will never ever forget you, ever." I said with tears in my eyes.

"Time to board!" yelled the coachman

"What will you do Dilk?" I quickly asked him.

"Ohh I'll keep on traveling I guess."

"Travelling?" He didn't go anywhere I thought.

"Yes, I'm a traveler. I was passing through when Nastasia told me you needed looking after. Nastasia is a traveler too. We busk from place to place to see the world."

"Oh, I thought you were homeless... like me." I giggled

"Homeless, by choice. Go now. You take care okay. The streets are not for little girls."

With that, I boarded the coach and sat at a window facing Dilk. We waved to one another until we could no longer see the other.

$\infty\infty\infty$

The coach grew hotter after a couple of hours. There was not an empty seat, but thankfully there was a toilet. The coach did make one stop, but I don't know where, as I didn't get off. After several more hours, I was awoken to the coachman standing over me trying to wake me, to tell me that I had reached my destination.

Chapter Twenty Nine

Through the letterbox

I t was a long walk from Worthing seafront to Lancing in the dark. My feet hurt, and I was cold, and hungry by the time I finally reached the front door of a familiar house that was once my home. I was scared to ring the doorbell, and I didn't want to go to the back door as it was see-through. So instead I peered quietly through the letterbox. My heart was hammering in my chest. I could see my mother in the kitchen, she was pacing around, and talking to someone on the telephone.

"She's been seen" and several other garbled words, which I couldn't hear. "No, I'm not going looking. The police have told me to stay here in case she turns up, and they are on their way here."

All the while mum was talking, all I wanted to do was ring the bell and when she answered, just throw my arms around her, and tell her how much I loved and missed her. But the police were coming. They wanted to take me back to Pappy's! No, I wouldn't go I thought frantically. I had to hide! Quickly!.

I ran around to the back of the house, there was a narrow graveled road, which led to several garages. I climbed up into a tree and then onto one of the roughly felt garage roofs. I waited, trying to keep as low as I possibly could, as I didn't want to be seen by the neighbors on the other side of the garages. I felt afraid. I knew I should have run to the stables, and hidden in one of the empty stalls, or the big hay barn. However, the longing to be near my mother was so strong, that I just couldn't leave. I decided to hide and wait for the police to come and then leave again before I went to see her.

I could then hear the sound of a helicopter, and then I saw it's long searchlight shining over houses and gardens. As if that wasn't enough I saw flashing blue lights everywhere, coming down the road behind me and somewhere off to the side where my mother's house was.

I lay down on my tummy, my heart beating so fast! I was unable to hide anywhere else. Why didn't I try and get into the shed in mums back garden!? I screamed inside my head. There was no time, no time!

Suddenly I heard footsteps on the gravel road beneath. I was too scared to peer over, in case I was seen.

"Evie, I know you're up there" Called a males deep voice, and my body... froze.

I could hear something breaking the branches in the tree in which I had climbed earlier, to get onto the roof.

"I'm not coming down!" I called out. "So don't come up. Please leave me alone I just want to see my mother."

"I know. Look why don't you come on down off that roof. It's not safe up there. Come on, I will take you to see your mum." He pleaded. "You must be hungry. All I have is a lollypop, but it's yours to keep if you come down."

I stayed frozen on my belly. I wanted to see mum, what if he was telling the truth and he let me see her? or what if she just wanted them to say that so that they could take me away... back to Pappy's. I would never go back there. NEVER!. So I stayed quiet. I guess I was just hoping that he would get tired of trying to get me to come down and just leave me alone, but he didn't.

I was too busy listening to the policeman and the thoughts racing around inside my head that I didn't notice another policeman sneaking up on me.

"I've got her!" The policeman who had snuck up on me called out to the one below.

I was caught, and I had nowhere to run. I could not escape even if I tried, there were just too many of them.

With their help, I got down off the garage roof and I was taken to a waiting police car outside my mother's house. I could see her staring out at me, through the window. I couldn't tell what she was thinking or feeling. To be honest I could barely see her properly for my eyes had blurred with tears, which threatened to brim over at any moment.

I don't remember how long I sat in the back of the police car, or the journey to a small bungalow not far from my mother's house. I don't even remember being taken by a couple up into a room with bunk beds. I know one thing... many months went by before I saw my mother again.

Chapter Thirty

Bounced around

Over the next four years, I experienced many temporary foster homes and children's home's. I went through periods of anger, self-loathing, hatred, fear, and deep depression. I started smoking when I was twelve, and when I was thirteen I began wearing lots of make-up. I became rebellious, arguing back and forth with my foster carers, refusing to go to school. One of my school friends managed to get a bottle of Vodka, and I got so drunk. I ended up sitting in afternoon assembly completely off my face from the vodka. I got expelled. I was then home-tutored for a while until I got bored with that and I ended up taking off early in the mornings before my foster carers woke up, in a bid to avoid everyone, the tutor included.

∞∞∞

My dad visited me a few times. He didn't know how to really deal with me, I don't think anyone really did. I didn't want to talk with anyone about anything. I didn't want to keep living in foster homes, especially the ones in which they had children of their own, because no matter how much they tried to include me I just never fit in.

I saw my mother a few times, and the need that I had felt to have her in my life had faded somewhat. My mother had eventually left Derek and Lucy, and she went to live with her new boyfriend; Simon whom she had been having an affair with.

By the time I was due to turn sixteen, everyone had practically given up on trying to "fix me" and I ended up going to live with my mother and Simon in their two bedroomed flat, near the seafront.

I left school without sitting my exams, and I got three jobs. I worked weekends at newsagents, and in the evenings on the weekend I worked in a kebab shop, and through the week I worked in a fish and chip shop.

After a few months mum and Simon had broken up, and she left me with him.

One day Simon told me that he was giving up the flat to move somewhere else, and my mum ended up going to the local housing authority and getting a two-bedroomed chalet for us on a seafront caravan park. It's where a lot of people lived whilst waiting for a council house. My mother by this time had another new boyfriend his name was Phillip, and So I ended up moving into the chalet, alone.

I hated being there alone, especially at night. It was so dark, and windy, being close to the sea. There were around a hundred or so chalets close together. They were so close that you could hear muffled conversations or their televisions through the thin fabricated walls. Arguments, alcohol, and drugs were rife. I had been offered a joint on more than one occasion, not that I ever did. Drugs did not interest me.

∞∞∞

Eventually, of course, the council got wind that my mother was not living with me at the chalet, on one of their inspections, and I was served with eviction. I ended up going to live with mum and Phillip, and Phillip's older son Nathan in his two bedroomed flat.

My mother put me up on a camp bed in the living room. Thankfully I was only there in the evenings. I found Phillip's son, Nathan quite creepy. I would often catch him staring at me. He was always overly nice, offering to make me a cup of coffee, or keeping me awake in the living room every night trying to talk to me. I was always polite to Nathan though. I did feel a little sorry for him, as he never went out, had girlfriends or any friends that I knew of. I tried not to linger in a room that he was also in for too long though. It wasn't anything he did, it was more his disposition, and he made me feel uncomfortable. I did try my best a few times, trying to give him the benefit of the doubt, and that maybe not all men were the same as the ones I had encountered. I was wrong...

Chapter Thirty-One

Roses and obsession

I had just woken up when my mother called me into the kitchen.

"Evie, there is a card here for you and a red rose."

Really I thought, not knowing who could possibly be hand delivering a card with a rose on Valentine's Day? I wasn't dating anyone, and I had absolutely no interest in dating anyone. This had to be some sort of a joke.

I opened the large red envelope and pulled out the overly glittered card. To the one I love it said on the front. There was some sort of a love verse, and it was signed Love an admirer.

I was not a vain girl in any sense of the word, but at sixteen I was told many times by various people "what a beautiful girl I was." I was slender with long blonde hair full of curls. I took care in my appearance and had taken to wearing a little less make-up, and I dressed a lot more sensibly. I knew I looked older than Sixteen, as on many occasions I was served with cigarettes and my mother's alcohol.

On the way home from work one day a car stopped in a layby just ahead of me, and a man inside called me over. I thought he was going to ask me for directions or something when he said to me...

"I've been driving past you every day for a few months, and I know this is probably weird me doing this, but you are so beautiful, and I wondered if you would like to go on a date with me?."

Jesus! Was this man for real? How was I supposed to respond? My first thought was that he was a real creepy weirdo, trying to get me in his car, and then he said...

"Can I take you out to dinner?"

"Where do you work?" was all I could think. I wanted to know where this guy went every day to see me.

"I'm a pilot. I work at Shoreham airport. I'm on my way home, but I saw you and I had to stop, you see I've been trying to pluck up the courage to ask you out."

"I'm sorry I don't know how old you are, but I'm only sixteen, and I have to get home." I walked away without looking back, and I never saw him again.

I wondered if that man had maybe followed me home, and sent the card and rose. My mum put the rose I had left on the kitchen counter in a glass of water, but the card I put in my bag.

That night everyone had gone to bed, and I was tired from being on my feet at work all night, so I did the same.

I awoke to a hand stroking my face. It was dark, and the living room door which I always shut when going to bed was ajar. I sat bolt upright in bed, the hand moved, and I saw a figure get up from beside me and running out of the living room door. I knew from the outline that it was Nathan.

Before I had gotten out of bed I heard Nathan's bedroom door shut. I was physically shaking, not with fear or upset, but with rage. How dare he! How fucking dare he! That is it! I thought angrily.

I didn't bother knocking on his door since I knew he was

awake, probably sitting in there like the dirty coward he was. I threw open his door, and there was Nathan sitting on his bed... crying.

"How dare you come into the place where I sleep and put your dirty fucking hands on me" I hissed at him.

He got up, brushing my arm as he shut the bedroom door, leaving me in the room alone, with him.

"I'm sorry." He touched my face.

"Get your hand off me," I said through gritted teeth. "What the hell do you think you were doing?"

"I love you. I just wanted to touch you. It was me, the card and the rose. I thought you would know it was me."

I wanted to slap him straight across his face. My body was shaking so full with adrenaline.

"So you think that gives you a right to sneak up on me and put your hands on me?"

Nathan tried to kiss me, and I began moving my head, to avoid his attempts.

"Stop it, Nathan!! get off me!" I hissed.

"I just want to be with you. I know you love me too, I know you do." He pleaded in a whiney voice.

"I don't love you, Nathan, trust me. I'm sorry I don't feel that way." I hissed again.

The last thing I needed was to have to leave with nowhere to go in the middle of the night. I wanted to organize something in the morning because there was no way I was going to spend another night in this flat with him.

"You do love me, Evie. I know you do. Please say you love me." Nathan continued pleading.

I spotted a pint glass filled with water on a set of drawers beside me. I picked it up and threw the water at his face. He looked shocked.

I used that opportunity to leave his room.

Thirty-Two

I must be crazy

The very next day I had a chat with a friend, and I made the decision to stay with her for a while, at least until I could afford a place of my own. I was leaving the village cafe, after having a coffee and some toast; it was preferable to being at the flat when I bumped into Derek.

He greeted me kindly. I hadn't seen him in so long; it had been almost five years. The last person I wanted to be confronted with was him. My sister Lucy was living with him, and if it wasn't for that I probably would have kept walking, but I didn't.

He was very chatty and somewhat polite. I was a little shocked. I expected to meet with well, if I'm honest... an asshole. Instead, he seemed quite chirpy, but a little bit down in the dumps, nothing like the man who had tormented me for years as a small child. I didn't know if he ever knew what his best friend had done to me for all those years. I doubt I would ever have gotten the truth anyway. My heart though was still hardened to him. It was hard to feel sorry for someone who reveled in my pain.

"Can I get you a cuppa?" he asked me forlornly.

"I don't want anything. I'm just going to see a friend. I replied, hoping that he would just say goodbye.

"well if we are going the same way I'll walk with you?" He

asked with raised brows.

Bloody hell, someone somewhere really had it in for me. I remember thinking. Why could I not just have my breakfast and go about my life in peace!

I didn't say that though, I just nodded my head and began walking with my hands pushed deep into my coat pockets.

"I've been talking with your mother, and we are getting a divorce. She will realize one day how stupid she is and probably ask to come back." He said sadly.

"Really? Well, she never says anything to me about it soo..."

"I'm working on the trains now as a conductor, and the shifts are all over the place. I've asked her to help out with Lucy, but she can't because she's working in that nursing home up the road."

"How is Lucy?" I asked hopefully.

"She's good... she's in middle school now you know?" He said taking a swift sideways peek at me. "You are all grown up now, you're looking really nice, what are you doing with yourself now?"

I told him about my jobs and said that I was trying to find a place of my own.

"You can always come and stay with me and Lucy? You can have your old room back, and help me out with her. You won't have to pay anything. I work nightshifts more than anything though, so it will be good for her, you just being there."

My first thought was to tell him to get lost. Then I thought of Lucy, she would be about 11 years old by now. Lucy didn't know me though; I hadn't seen her in years. I couldn't go to Derek's house I thought. I felt like I wanted to cry. I didn't realize how much I wanted to see her, to talk to her until he brought her up. I looked at Derek, and he was looking at me expectantly, and sort of hopeful.

I hadn't realized that we had stopped walking. It was hard to see him acting and talking to me like I was an old friend after everything he had done to me. All I had ever wanted was for him to if not love me, then at least like me and to be kind. All my thoughts and emotions were all over the place.

I was torn between wanting to see Lucy, and not wanting to be under the same roof as this man. Torn because I had always wanted him to treat me as if I was someone, and not something, and at this moment there was nothing of the man in him I had grown to hate.

I thought of my own situation at the flat, and going to live on a friend's sofa, and I thought about living under the same roof with the man before me. My first option was the friend's sofa, and then the power to see Lucy again was overpowering all other thoughts.

"I'll bring my stuff over later." Oh my god, what had I said. I really had not thought any of this through. I must be crazy!

Chapter Thirty-Three

Mistaken Identity

I had been living with Derek and Lucy for a few weeks. It was difficult having to sleep in my old room with all those terrible memories of Melvin Sexually abusing me. It helped that the room had been re-decorated in neutral colors, with darker curtains as opposed to Carebears. The bed was in a different place, as was a brand new set of drawers. Lucy and I got re-acquainted, and I enjoyed helping and watching her coloring in, making cakes and taking her to see my now very old pony, Poppy. I didn't have time to pop up to the stables very often anymore, but it was nice watching her enjoying sitting on horseback as much as I used to, well after she got over her initial fear anyway. I barely saw Derek in fact, as he worked nights and I worked days, so after seeing Lucy off to school, and by the time I got home, Derek would be ready to set off.

On my Saturdays off I would meet some friends at the local village pub for a game of pool. It was a something I had done every week for the past few months. I knew the owners and they were pretty cool with letting me in for a few games of pool, whilst listening to the jukebox.

That night for some reason I walked a different way home, instead of under the railway bridge I decided to walk the long way. In a way, I'm glad I did.

There was a frantic knocking at the door the next morning, it was my mother.

"Quick let me in I need to talk to you, It's about Nathan." My mum looked halfway hysterical as I let her in and went to sit in the dining room.

"Nathan attacked a woman last night under the railway bridge and she thought he was going to try and rape her. He tried getting her on the floor and he was trying to get her trousers off!" my mothers' hand was shaking on her forehead.

"Okay calm down," I said, as I put the kettle on to make her a cup of tea. Once she had her tea, and I had my coffee I joined her at the dining table.

"Is the woman okay? And who was she?" I asked worriedly, but still trying to wipe the sleep from my eyes. Lancing at the time was only a small village, where everyone knew everyone, and anything that happened publicly was never a secret for very long.

"It was Denise from across the road from here. She was walking home from the British Legion when she noticed she was being followed. All I know from the police who came knocking at our door at one o clock this morning was that Nathan had been arrested. Oh my god, he attacked her!"

I knew Denise, not personally, but she had lived across the road for years, she was a nice lady.

"That's awful. Is she okay though?" I asked forlornly.

"Is she okay, yes, yes, but Evie... Nathan told the police that he thought it was you, and he tried to say it was all a joke, but it wasn't! it was supposed to be you he kept shouting as they arrested him!"

Oh my god, I thought. I felt pins and needles in my cheeks and I felt ice cold water was running through my veins, instead of warm blood.

"Denise managed to fight him off and run, but she told the police that someone needed to warn you."

"Last night I was at the pub, and I walked a different way home," I told her.

"Denise looks a bit like you from behind, he must have thought she was you." My mother muttered, looking a lot calmer.

"Where is Nathan now?" I asked, holding my breath, waiting for an answer.

"He's still at the station; he's got to go to court. It will be in the paper, and Phillip is standing by him."

I released my breath in a low whoosh through my gritted teeth, and then I told her about Nathan creeping into the living room at the flat, the card, the rose... everything.

"Why the bloody hell didn't you tell me? She asked, looking shocked.

"Would anyone have cared?" to be honest I never felt right when he was around."

"He's completely obsessed with you Evie. Don't come back to the flat whatever you do, though I doubt that he's stupid enough to try anything else. He was crying on the phone to Phillip."

"Well, he deserves everything he bloody well gets." I snapped.

Later on that day I made my way over to see Denise. Her eyes looked a little puffy and swollen from I imagined crying, and lack of sleep. I thanked her for the warning, and I said I was sorry that she had to experience what she had, and had to go through with the police. I explained what he had been doing and saying to me whilst I was living in the flat.

I stopped going out after that, afraid to see him, afraid that he would be waiting again under the shadows of the bridge.

Chapter Thirty-Four

A New Career

For the next year, I devoted myself to becoming a carer for the elderly. I got a full-time job at a carehome in Hove, East Sussex, and one evening a week I went to Brighton college for my folder work and exams. Every week an assessor would come to the care home, and observe me in my duties, such as feeding a resident, bathing or dressing them, and such.

∞∞∞

Sunday's would be my day off and I would sometimes take one of the elderly ladies out for Sunday dinner, as she didn't have any family, and she was one of my favorites. I would rather have spent time with her and hearing about her life during world war two than I would have sitting in a pub somewhere watching my mates getting drunk. It was during my time working at the care home that I had developed a softer side. I was no longer this angry person. I spent day in, and day out with the elderly, helping them to do the things they no longer could. I developed a deep humility. I loved hearing about their lives. I realized that there was soo much more to them, than little old people sitting in chairs all day, just merely existing. Their lives were once so different and it was interesting to me.

They taught me many things, just by talking to me, and they really gave me a lot to really think about sometimes. I went from breezing in and out of their rooms when my jobs were done to sitting down and talking to them, not just talking but really listening, and enjoying their company. I spent soo much time talking with them that I thought someone was sure to say something, and I would get fired. Nobody said anything though, and when it came to home-time, sometimes I would stay on and read someone a letter, or make them an extra cup of tea, and others I would take out in their wheelchairs for fresh air.

There was this one cheeky old chap Harry. Harry was a smoker, and back then they were allowed to smoke in their rooms. Every now and then I would nip in to see him, and have a cheeky smoke myself. Harry was always talking about the war. He had been a soldier and he told me what it was like in the muddy, wet trenches, and that he almost died when a bomb dropped into the trench, luckily he was in a room built inside, however the beams came down trapping him underneath, and the water was rising fast with the rain. He told me that he almost drowned, and if it wasn't for another group of soldiers coming along he probably would have perished.

The home that I worked in was actually a two house care home. The elderly home where I worked was in one house, and it had a connecting door into the second house, which was a home for residents with Down's syndrome.

I learned that many of these lovely people were given up at birth, and their families paid to have them looked after in the home and that most of the families didn't even bother to visit, let alone send them cards or gifts on birthdays or Christmas. They were all so wonderful, loving and many of them seemed very happy.

Once I had gotten over my initial sadness for them I realized that I had no right to feel that way just because they looked different and acted differently. They were in fact just like anyone else, with thoughts and feelings. To me, they were pure souls, and well... beautiful people. I loved every minute spent with them watching movies, making cakes, singing and dancing. I loved every single one of them, and I would have been happy to move into that house myself! I couldn't do that of course, but I did switch to working there full time instead. I didn't think of them as residents, they were my friends. I made them birthday cakes if I knew one of them had a birthday, and I even wrapped them little presents. I would turn the music up on the radio and dance, and jump around with them, and do you know what? They were the most honest to goodness people that I had ever met in my life.

Chapter Thirty-Five

Go on take a Chance

A few of my friends from work had been encouraging me for a few months to go on the dating scene. Going out with some random, unknown guy was just not my thing. Nobody knew what I had been through, it wasn't something you just volunteer to someone, and besides I worked almost seventy hours a week, I had no time to date!

Maybe I wasn't forceful enough about it because one day Steph a fellow carer at work had approached me full of excitement.

"I've put an advert in the dating section of the Friday-Ad, but don't worry they have to call a number and leave you a message, and they leave you a number to call them... if you are interested. At least you will know what they sound like, and hear a bit about them." She said rather quickly.

All I could do was frown, as I carried on folding the bedsheets.

"Look, you don't have to speak to anyone... unless you like the sound of them. Plus you can meet them in a public place, so you will feel safe."

"I don't know Steph. It's a bit risky don't you think?" I looked at her dubiously.

"Urgh, life is a risk. You're a beautiful girl, wasting away in this place! Sometimes you have to take a chance. If you don't then you may never find your Mr. Right." She said eyebrows raised, and a silly grin on her face.

I took the paper from her now outstretched hand.

"Eighteen!, you said I'm eighteen. I'm seventeen Steph. I can't even wash a bare bum in this place without supervision." I had to wait until I was fully qualified and eighteen before I was allowed to deal with the residents personal needs alone.

"Well you had to be eighteen to post an advert, and well you can sort that out later if you find someone you like. Just say it was a mistake... or whatever!"

Ohh-my- god I thought, this whole thing just sounded crazy, not to mention completely embarrassing.

"This is the number to call for your inbox messages," Steph said handing me a crumpled bit of paper from her apron pocket.

It was late evening when I got home, and everyone was fast asleep. Thankfully since I had started working full time at the care home, Derek had managed to change his shifts around, and a parent of one of Lucy's friends would help to look after Lucy around our work shifts.

I almost had enough money saved for a deposit for a flat of my own, as well as some funds for furnishing it. I did find it a struggle to save, I worked so hard, but most of my money was taken up with traveling from Lancing to Hove by train every day, and takeaways. I never seemed to find time to cook for myself, it was a constant eat and run, except for Sundays when I went out with the little old lady from work, but even then that came out of my wages to. I sighed.

The conversation with Steph that morning was playing on my mind. I guess I was beginning to feel lonely. Some of my friends were blissfully happy in their relationships, whilst others were constantly complaining about how terrible their relationships were. I didn't really want any relationship drama. I couldn't see the point in staying in one if I was miserable all the time. As for the ones who were happy, I was slightly envious. I did see a guy for a little while but it just didn't work out.

To me, relationships just seemed like some sort of emotional minefield. I didn't know if I was ready. I had been through so much. What if they wanted some nice girl with a wonderful home and a non-dysfunctional family? Instead, they were going to get a girl with an alcoholic mother and father, a stepfather that physically and emotionally abused her, yet – she still lives with him. To top it off I was sexually ruined as a child, and because of that, I spent my life bouncing from one foster home to another.

I made myself a cup of coffee, lit a cigarette and sat at the dining room table. I came to quickly realize that I was not actually someone that would be ideal as a date. I had too much emotional baggage that I was unable to just simply discard. It's not something I could just forget, or move on from. It was there when I closed my eyes when I showered when I looked at myself in a mirror when I worked. It was when I looked at my family; it was in everything, and everywhere. I carried my pain like a deeply invisible scab, a scab that wouldn't heal.

I managed to find a kind of peace and comfort in the care home's being surrounded by people who were in some way as helpless as I sometimes felt. That may sound awful, but I mean in the sense that their minds would sometimes wander between a life they once had and a life that they lived now. Maybe they were at peace with not having to battle with their families, or be a go-between, or struggle to pay bills and cook dinner on time. They were just there, living in their memories, like I.

I had made the decision to work hard and be independent. As a small child, you rely on adults to take care of you, and the adults let me down, and well… I didn't want to have to ever rely on anyone but myself. I didn't want anyone. I was going to be a happy spinster; well I would maybe get a dog or a cat someday.

Nope, I thought I was going to stay true and firm to my original plan, and with that, I took my tired form off to bed.

Chapter Thirty-Six

Curiosity

C uriosity got the better of me though. I couldn't help by wonder if someone had left me a message in my newly created dating inbox, thanks to Steph. It couldn't do any harm I procrastinated, and so I dialed the number. I had three messages, for which I listened to them all. Out of the three, I liked the sound of the second one, he had a soft voice. His name was Andrew, and he was seven years older than me, making him twenty-four years old. Andrew was a builder in a family business, and from Newhaven, East Sussex. I hesitated on whether I should call him or not. I was really scared. Nope I was going to work, and off I went.

∞∞∞

I told Steph about the messages and Andrew, a little later on at work. I told her how nervous I was, and that I was concerned about the slight age gap. I thought that he may be the type to want to settle down, get married, and have kids. I didn't know if I was ready for any of that so soon.

"Just call him. You are making assumptions about the guy, that you have never even met." She proclaimed.

It wasn't until the next day that I decided to call his number. My hand felt clammy on the phone, and my mouth felt dry.

What in the world was I going to say? What if we were stuck for conversation? I thought of a million and one ways this whole call would end in disaster, and then he answered the phone, and... I hung up.

My hands were shaking, and I could feel a headache coming on. Then the phone rang.

"Hello?" I spoke into the receiver.

"Hi, I just had a call but someone hung up." Said a friendly, male voice.

Holy hell, this was Andrew! Shit, shit I thought.

"Hello, are you still there?"

"Yes, um sorry It was me. I didn't mean to hang up. I j just didn't know what to say to you."

"Hang on, do I know you?" he asked curiously.

"Um, yes, no, well you left a message in my dating inbox and I thought I would call you."

Andrew seemed to put me at ease with his soft, easy tone, after my initial embarrassment of hanging up on him, and we agreed to meet in a public place for a coffee the following day.

I actually ended up in his car on the way to Newhaven where Andrew lived, with his parents.

His parents were older, and they had three other sons, a daughter, as well as six grandchildren. They were all very family orientated, and everyone seemed to be really nice.

I wouldn't say I immediately fell in love with Andrew. He

seemed to sort of love himself quite a bit, and he was some-times a little too over confident for my liking, however he also came across as friendly, and quite bubbly. He was very atten-tive taking me out to dinner, to pubs, and involving me in all of his family gatherings.

Sometimes when we were out he would make quite deroga-tory or disparaging remarks about people that he didn't know know though, and that put me off him a little.

I grew very fond of his parents, quite often they would tell me that I should get a job locally, and move in with them, to save Andrew driving to lancing every other day to pick me up, for only a few hours before having to drive me back home again.

I was fond of Andrew, but I was still at the getting to know him stage and moving in with him and his family was not some-thing that I was comfortable with. I guess I felt too polite to say no. I didn't want to offend them, or for Andrew to think that I was losing interest. It was more a fear of intimacy and moving too fast.

Chapter Thirty-Seven

An unexpected visitor

By the third month, I ended up moving in with Andrew in his parents' house, and he had in a way asked me to get engaged. It was nothing like you see in the movies... when a guy sweeps the girl off her feet in a wave of romance, and gets down on one knee, declaring his forever love. It was "we could get engaged... or not. We already live together."

I tried clinging to his tender moments, as opposed to his darker ones when he would say derogatory things about the way I dressed, wore my hair, and who I spoke to. I began to take the things that he said to me on board. I think because he was seven years older, I thought of him as wiser. He made me feel like I needed to be more mature. He told me I was naïve because I didn't know certain things that he did, or that I didn't respond to things the way he would.

Maybe, I thought, he was right. Maybe life wasn't like the movies, maybe this is what it was really like, and maybe you are supposed to "better each other" over time.

I think I fell in love with his family, more than I did with Andrew. His mother was kind, caring and she loved all of her family so fiercely, and she was the same with me.

As for Andrew's father, I was shocked to find myself feeling so comfortable around him. He wasn't a man of great words, but he was a relaxed person, he enjoyed a giggle with me, and he was hard working.

Their house was always so full, and the walls would ring with their laughter, and kindly chiding. It would have been perfect if I could only feel for Andrew the way I wanted to.

I know I held myself back a lot, because I felt uncomfortable with a lot of kissing, even having him touch my body was difficult, but I wanted so much to be comfortable with him, and well normal. I did eventually manage to pluck up the courage to tell him about Melvin, after a couple of weeks when he tried getting more serious with me. I didn't feel it was right to not tell him. I thought that if I didn't, maybe he would think my aversions were towards him as opposed to my past.

∞∞∞

The day before I told him I had a visit from a lady from the social services department or some such. In her hands was a thick padded brown envelope, to which she handed to me.

The lady explained that it was my case notes or reports to do with the sexual abuse I was subjected to. I had only ever given one statement, and that was it. I had never heard anything until that day.

"Your files will be archived and I wanted to bring these documents to you. I thought you should read them."

"I don't understand," I responded more shocked at this lady turning up with some files and awful reminders.

"I think you need to have this looked into again Evie. I know they said there was not enough evidence to charge him...."

"Well, their bloody well wouldn't be any would there? I half shouted. "He didn't exactly shove his hand in my knickers in front of anyone!"

"No. I know that Evie. Sadly there is never enough evidence to convict pedophiles; it's always the victim's words against the accused. Unless there is a witness or physical evidence, then there is no case."

"So basically he continues to walk free." I half sobbed.

"Evie has nobody ever told you?" she frowned in deep concern.

"No. I haven't spoken to anyone, and not one person has ever spoken of it to me."

"Have you not had any counseling or anything like that?" she asked.

"No," I answered flatly, swallowing my pain.

"The reason I came is that in the report, Melvin made a rather incriminating statement, but at the time he was with a single officer and he was not under caution."

"Thank you for the documents. I don't know what good they are to me, but I appreciate your time." I stood and walked towards the front door, hoping the lady would follow me. She did.

I skimmed the pages when she had gone. What could I do? He was free, that's all I was left with, besides all this painful paperwork.

∞∞∞

The next day I told Andrew. I didn't know what I expected him to say but it wasn't "and why are you telling me, or showing me this stuff?"

"Well, you're better off without your family in my opinion." Was all he said, and that was the end of the matter.

A couple of days after that is when he began making his disparaging remarks towards me. Maybe it was shock, or disgust in me, I couldn't decide, maybe he needed time.

Now after a few months of living with him and his family, and feeling accepted, and a part of their family. I found myself muttering

"Okay" In response to an engagement proposal. I never received an engagement ring, not for a long, long while.

Chapter Thirty-Eight

Decisions, decisions

Andrew's parents had organized an engagement party for Andrew, and I. I wasn't as happy as I had hoped or expected to feel, at the prospect of celebrating our future matrimony. I tried my very best to open up to him and be romantic, but what was in his eyes when we first met had changed. It felt like he wanted me physically, but not emotionally.

A few days before the party Andrew took me for a drive to Newhaven fort, so we could sit facing the sea, and enjoy the view.

"I need you to do something for Me," he asked a little sheepishly, at the same time he gently squeezed my hand within his between the seats.

"I'm married to someone called Beth, and we are in the process of a divorce, and she's being difficult about signing the papers. I wondered if you would call her for me now, and tell her who you are and that we plan to marry, and ask her to sign the divorce papers."

Oh my god he's a married man. Was all I could think. He never said, and nobody else had ever mentioned he had a wife to me either! One thing was for sure I was not going to ring up his wife and tell her to sign the papers. I was not brave, and I didn't feel that was right.

"I can't Andrew. I don't know her. Why didn't you tell me?"

"Because I thought she would sign the papers, and it would be all over and done with by now."

I expected him to apologize for not telling me about Beth, but he didn't.

"Don't bother then, I'll deal with her myself." He half spat.

How could I be engaged to a man while he was still bloody married?!

When we got back to his house I ran upstairs and shut myself in our bedroom and cried myself to sleep on the bed.

I didn't see Andrew until the next day, and all he said to me was "It's sorted."

Two days later I was all done up, wearing a dress, and sitting at a table surrounded by Andrew's family, and a few of my friends. It was supposed to be happy, we were supposed to be happy and in love. Instead, he was off laughing with his mates on one side, and I was sat at a table surrounded by his family, and all I wanted to do was cry. I didn't want it to be like this. I didn't want us to be like this.

I had two choices. One I could stay with him, and try to accept the fact that he may be finding it difficult to be with someone, having had such a dysfunctional life. I did care for him; almost love him I thought, especially when he was in a loving mood towards me, and when he said nice things. Maybe love grows stronger over time for some people? I was thinking. I did feel safe with him, and to me, that counted for a lot.

Or option two I could call off the engagement and get my old job back at the care home in Hove. I had enough money saved to at least get myself a nice studio apartment on Lancing sea-front. I could go back to my original plan and become an old spinster.

∞∞∞

All night I fought with my feelings, weighing the options. Andrews's parents seemed genuinely fond of me and made a big thing of Andrew being happy and settled, and almost making out that I was the best thing since sliced bread! Oh my, how could I hurt them? or Andrew? What if he would be really hurt deep down? What if I would be throwing away the chance of future happiness? Was I being too greedy in wanting my future husband to be good to me all of the time?

One thing I was sure of was that I didn't want anyone to be hurt.

I decided to see the night through, and to take my time making on making a decision, because as far as I was concerned... this was a lifetime commitment.

Chapter Thirty-Nine

Afraid to stay, afraid to leave

Towards the end of the engagement party, Andrew had managed to down several pints. He was singing, holding me, kissing me and it felt wonderful. I myself had had several glasses of wine. I felt so relaxed, and out of my shell more than I had ever been in my entire life! Which was unusual, but looking back I was not a drinker, and it didn't take very long at all for me to shrug off my inhibitions.

That night we made love. I was shocked at my new confidence I was exuding. I felt comfortable with my body, and what was happening between us. I completely let myself go.

The next morning I awoke with a blinding headache, and I wanted to be sick, and I was totally and utterly naked! I had never before been completely naked with him, and that bothered me more than my pounding head, and gurgling tummy.

I managed to sneak out of bed, grab a bathrobe and run downstairs, past the kitchen to the bathroom, and it was then that I lost the entire contents of my stomach.

Andrew seemed a little happier than usual, and I was feeling depressed that I couldn't enjoy his new mood due to how ill I was for the rest of the day, which I had to spend in darkness, with the curtains drawn, and my head buried under a pillow.

∞∞∞

The next day I was well enough to begin my first ever night shift at a new nursing home nearby, and over the three to four weeks we made love several more times. I didn't feel as free-spirited as the night of the engagement, but it was a little easier, and I had decided to give our relationship my all.

It was towards the end of the week when we went for a meal with his parents at a little local restaurant called Benbows that everything went from zero to one hundred in a downward spiral.

Andrew had begun insulting me over an opinion I had. I don't remember exactly what it was about, but I do remember that he shamed me in front of his parents and the entire restaurant, and for that, I was mortified. I felt like a young child again being scalded by Derek at the dinner table. I remained seated, feeling the silence, as well as several pairs of eyes fixed on me. I sucked in my breath and tried to hold back the tears that blurred my vision. A searing hot ball of pain burned in my throat, at the torrent of tears that I was holding back. My hands trembled as I forced myself to cut the meat on my plate, and the fork shook as I brought the food up to my mouth. It was after this that Andrews parents had changed the subject and talked mostly amongst themselves for the next thirty or so minutes. The rest of the diners carried on also.

After the meal was finished with, well everyone's except mine because I struggled to eat it, we walked back to the house in silence, and once again for the third time in two days I was sick. I couldn't take it. I couldn't live like this; it was making me physically ill. I felt weak, tired and incredibly sad. Andrew was vicious in his statements, calling me a stupid bitch, a thick cow and oh the list went on. I snapped, I had, had enough. This is not how I wanted to spend my life, or with someone like him.

"We are finished, Andrew. I am leaving you." I yelled.

Andrew grabbed me by my arms and began squeezing them so hard.

"Get off me!" I shouted.

And then Andrew gave me a short, sharp slap across my cheek.

His mother came into the room at the same time that Andrew had slapped my face.

"Andrew! What is going on here?" she asked him, looking quite mollified as I stood there holding my face. Andrew did in fact look more than a little contrite.

"Sorry Mum, we had an argument." he said sheepishly, as he began to usher her from the room. encouraging her to go downstairs with him.

Chapter Forty

I'm sorry. It won't happen again

That night I slept alone, and Andrew slept on the sofa in the living room. It was too late for transport that night and I had no choice but to stay. My plan was to get a quick shower in the morning, get dressed, and then pack my things. Before I got to the stage where I could pack my thing's Andrew timidly entered the bedroom.

"Please don't leave me. I'm sorry. It won't happen again." He pleaded.

I looked into his blue eyes and downturned mouth, he did look sorry. He looked like he was trying very hard not to cry.

"I can't live like this Andrew. I don't think that we are right for each other at all. We are two very different people. It was a mistake to let it go this far." I said softly, and feeling as if all the fight I had earned over the last few years had left my body.

"Please just listen to me. My dad is giving me more responsibility at work, and I found us a house. It was meant to be a surprise. I've been feeling all kinds of pressure lately, and I took it out on you. It will never, never happen again. Please forgive me. I'll do anything." His voice was wobbly with trying not to cry, and he sounded like he was almost whining in his words.

"See Andrew this is a problem, you don't talk to me about things and I feel like I can't talk to you either. How on earth can we buy a home, and get married after everything you said to me last night, and after you slapped me!" I began to cry. "I thought I was safe with you!"

"I'm sorry." Andrew sat on the bed, and he too began sobbing. He tried pulling me by the waist towards him.

I let him hold me and bury his face into my waist. He took my loose arms that were by my sides to hold him as if I were a mother comforting a small child. I felt his wracking sobs, it felt as if they were absorbing into me, and joining with my own.

"You will never, ever strike me again Andrew. If you do or threaten to, then I will leave you."

∞∞∞

It was upsetting to see him crying, looking defenseless, and weak. I knew those feelings all too well, the fear of losing someone you love or care about, and it tugged at me.

It didn't stop my mind though from re-playing the previous evening events for the rest of that day, and night, over what he had said and done to me the night before. It made me cringe. I was slightly disappointed in my giving in so easily to him. Maybe I should have left, and taken things from there after a few days. I hoped I had made the right decision in giving him this one chance. I would never let him do that to me again.

I wanted to be in love with him. He was so lovely when he wasn't mad.

I missed my work friends from Hove, from that day onwards, hell I even missed my mother, what I used to see of her anyway. I hadn't been at my new job long enough to make any real friends there, so talking to anyone at work was out of the question.

Andrew changed though and once more he seemed like the man I had first met all over again. He was kind, loving, and very complimenting of the way I dressed or wore my hair.

But I was still sick. Each morning I awoke with an imminent feeling that I was going to throw up what little I was managing to keep down. I was tired and had slight cramping. Despite this, we arranged to look at a two bedroomed house in Newhaven. It was about a five-minute drive from his parents' house, and still close to the small town.

Chapter Forty-One

Unexpected surprise

"Well congratulations Evie, you're pregnant." The female doctor with sort curly brown hair announced, looking at me with a big smile, and her finely arched eyebrows raised.

"Really? You're sure?" I asked because I was on the combined pill. I had been on it for years, and I had taken it every day religiously. I felt like everything has slowed right down, and it was as if my ears were stuffed with cotton wool because the doctor answered by I couldn't hear her very well. It was as if she was talking to me quietly from across a vast room, and then I heard her say...

"I take it, that this wasn't planned?" she asked turning her raised brows into a concerned frown.

"No... it wasn't planned. We have only just got engaged, and we have been arguing." There were a few moments of silence between us, and I tried to quickly absorb her words. "I am on the pill. I have not missed one day."

The doctor lightly smiled and patted my hand. "It's not a failsafe. You can still get pregnant. If you are unwell or on certain medications then that can disturb the effectiveness of the pill."

My mind began racing with thoughts of when I first started to get sick. "It was a few weeks ago, the morning after the engagement party. I was sick, then It went away, and then I got sick again." I said a little less numbly.

"Well, it's most likely that when you were sick the first time, that you lost the pill." She said matter of factly.

Yes, I took it later that day, after the buffet at the engagement party. I was in such a rush to get ready that I took it later. I drank all that wine, and of course, I threw up.

The doctor had asked me to cease taking the pill straight away, and she gave me several booklets on pregnancy. I was booked in for an appointment with the midwife to see how far along I was, and she advised me to begin taking folic acid.

I decided to call in sick at work for that evening, and I spent the rest of the day sitting by the beach reading the booklets and worrying about Andrew's reaction.

I chose not to say anything that night to Andrew. I needed the news to sink in properly before I could discuss anything. I was quiet, and all I could think about was the tiny new life taking form inside of me. The more I thought about it, the warmer I felt towards the baby, and the numbness I felt at first had turned to a bubble of happiness.

∞∞∞

The next day I still hadn't plucked up the courage to tell Andrew that I was pregnant, and I went to work in the nursing home that evening. I was called into the manager's office, as I guess she was a little concerned about the sick days I was having recently. I felt the need to explain, now that I knew what was causing me to feel so ill, and tired. I wasn't comfortable telling a boss that I hardly knew, before telling Andrew, but I felt that I had no choice. I didn't want to lose my job, which I truly did love.

But when I told her that I was pregnant, she told me how sorry she was, but she would have to terminate my employment. Apparently, their insurance did not cover pregnant women to work in the home, due to the heavy lifting of patients that is required and often necessary. They couldn't be responsible for anything untoward happening, such as a miscarriage if I were to do something that I shouldn't during pregnancy.

I understood what she was saying, but it felt so coldly put. Now I was going to have to tell Andrew that not only was I pregnant but that I had also just lost my job.

That evening Andrew and his parents were surprised to see me back, as I wasn't due back until the morning. I asked to speak with Andrew in our room. Here goes. I thought.

"Andrew I have been very ill for the past few weeks, and so I went to see the Doctor, and well... I'm pregnant. I've also lost my job at the nursing home, but I plan on getting another job as soon as possible."

"What do you mean you're pregnant? You are on the bloody pill." He said worriedly.

"Yes, I am.. or I was. It must have happened the night of our engagement party, as I got drunk, I was sick, and... we made love."

"I'm not very happy about this. What about you? You don't look worried." He asked with a deep frown.

"Well I was shocked at first, but I've had a chance to let it sink in, and no I'm not worried. I'm actually happy. I can't be mad about having a child Andrew. I'm sure it was going to happen one day, and I'll be eighteen.

"Jesus Christ!" Andrew exclaimed as he stood up. I couldn't

help my reaction, I flinched. I thought he was going to hit me, and my reaction did not go unnoticed. He looked angry, and his eyes were moving rapidly in what looked like quick thoughts. He grabbed hold of my hand and told me that we were going to tell his parents, in a way that said I was going to be in trouble with them.

Chapter Forty-Two

Playing card

I couldn't tell if his parents were happy or not at becoming grandparents to a seventh grandchild. They seemed very calm, maybe too calm. Why did I feel like I was in trouble for letting this happen? I would have liked children when we were married, living in a home of our own maybe, but the fact that we were already engaged and had a viewing date to look at a house wasn't to be an awful start I thought.

Andrew seemed to go from confrontational about the pregnancy, to somewhere after a brief silence quite morose. I was surprised when he looked at both of his parents and asked...

"I hope you won't treat us any differently now."

His question shocked me, for she didn't seem like the type of mother or grandmother that would turn her back on her child or her grandchild. His mother looked quite surprised too, and his father said...

"Of course we wouldn't," he said affectionately, but with also a little upset in his voice.

Why on earth would they treat us, or him differently? I wondered. Thing's had been a little strained after Andrew and I had the argument, but it was probably awkward for them having to hear it, and for his mum to witness it. As was her way through, she didn't bring it up, and after a day or so she was fine again.

"Thank you." Was all I could say to them as we left them in the living room.

As Andrew closed the bedroom door I decided to ask Andrew why? he had to ask his mum not to treat us differently.

"Ohh just because they are old fashioned, and with us not being married."

"No Andrew that's not why. Your older brother had twins with Amanda before they were married, and your parents were happy for them, or so they said." I knew I was being lied to, and I wanted to know the real reason.

Andrew gave in and explained that he was worried his dad would treat him differently now. Andrew was undoubtedly their favorite, it was no secret, and it was jokingly mentioned by his other family members on numerous occasions.

Andrew was now telling me that his father had been setting him up to take over the very lucrative, and successful family business, but he was worried now that his father would back out if he was to have a young family right now, and give the business to his older brother.

It dawned on me that he was more worried about his position, and not his child's. What he was really asking was for nothing to change with him, because I was pregnant. He was disgusting! I thought angrily.

I could tell them about your past, you know, and they would feel bad, especially Dad.

"You want to use my awful childhood experiences, as a playing card with your parents? To make them feel sorry for me... for you?

I felt anger bubbling up within me. I would not be painted as some sort of sad case. I was not a victim. I hated that word, it made me feel like a weak, useless person whenever I heard it, and I didn't need anyone to feel sorry for me! Not ever! And how dare he want to tell them! It was none of their business, and it was not his to tell anyone he pleased. I angrily thought.

I began to gather my clothes from the drawers beside the bed and stuffing them inside the suitcase that I pulled out from under the bed.

"You Andrew are more concerned about yourself in all this with your parents than you are with your wife-to-be and your child. You are selfish, cruel more than you are kind, and you have no right to tell anyone about what I went through." I spoke shakily but calmly, as I continued to pack my case. If my pregnancy inconveniences you then I will leave... I am more than happy to leave An asshole like you!

Bam! Andrew's fist came flying towards my head, knocking me to the floor on my side. I felt dazed and Andrew was yelling at me, but I couldn't make out what. His eyes were wide, and his mouth was trembling. He bent over me and I felt several hard slaps across my head. I couldn't register the pain. Why couldn't I feel the pain? I could hear the sounds the dull thuds about my head, and his fist making contact on my mouth, but I couldn't feel anything.

"If you leave you're not having that kid, you can get rid of it." I heard him hiss at me.

I didn't move. I daren't move. I kept my head downwards and put my hands on my head to protect his impacts. I waited, for what felt like hours. I was getting stiff, and my lip was beginning to sting. I couldn't stay like this. What if he hurt me too much? I could lose the baby.

I gathered what little courage I had, and raised myself up onto my knees, and I made my way over to the case.

I don't know if it was the sound of someone coming up the stairs to investigate, but he let me finish packing, and...he let me go.

Chapter Forty-Three

Breaking free

I managed to catch a late bus to Brighton, and from there I had to get a taxi to Lancing. I was back at Derek's. He was surprised to see me, but he didn't turn me away.

I was too exhausted to clean myself up; god only knows what I looked like. But I didn't really care. I never thought I would ever run to this house for safety. I fell into an exhausted sleep, and it was afternoon the following day when I woke up.

My head, nose, lip, and chin were agony.

The house was empty when I came down to make myself a coffee. I took it back upstairs and began running a warm bath. It was then that I looked in the mirror. My bottom lip was split, and my cheek, nose, and chin were pink and purple. I had dried blood encrusted inside my nose. I looked an absolute mess.

I managed to clean myself up, and I found some ointment in the bathroom cabinet. I hadn't managed to pack my makeup at Andrew's, so there was no covering it until I could get to Boots chemist in the village.

I could hear the telephone ringing several times downstairs. I ignored it.

I managed to get myself some foundation and powder from the chemist, as well as a red lipstick to cover the purple. I put as much as I could on without looking like an overpainted doll in the Library toilets, around the corner from boots. My bruising and lip were only faintly noticeable, and that was better than what it looked like before.

I then hopped onto a bus to Shoreham Council and waited for the rest of the day to see someone from the housing department. In order for them to house me I was put on a waiting list, and until something became available, they booked me into a bed and breakfast in an old Victorian townhouse along Worthing seafront, for the following night. Being a bed and breakfast I was told that I was not allowed to stay there during the day and that I would have to vacate by 9 am and not return till 5 pm. If I wasn't back by 11 pm then the door would be locked.

Derek informed me that evening that Andrew had been calling the house non-stop since he had gotten home, and that he had to unplug the phone cord from the wall socket, and he was not pleased about it. Neither would I have been if it was my phone I thought.

I told Derek that I was moving to a bed and breakfast the next day, and he could tell Andrew that he hadn't seen me. Derek agreed but offered me the use of the house during the days that I had to be out of the bed and breakfast. I could not fathom this man at all sometimes, but then I thought well I'm not a kid anymore and now he's suffered his own heartbreak with my mother leaving, so maybe I could. It still didn't make it right though, but I found it hard to hate him, as I once did.

The next morning I re-packed my case and hopped on the bus to Worthing town center, and I used some of my now precious savings to buy some non-perishable food items for the B&B. I managed to find the place relatively easily, and I rang the bell rather timidly.

A kindly plump lady with thick, red, curly hair answered the door. I introduced myself and asked if it would be okay to store my thing's somewhere until I could return at 5 pm. The lady was very kind and took my things, reassuring me that she would keep my things safe in her living area. I was then left with a few hours to fill, so I made my way to Worthing Pier and bought myself a cone of chips.

I called my Nan to check in and I told her that thing's hadn't worked out between Andrew and me, but that I was okay, and I promised to go and see her soon.

There was no way I could turn up at my Nans like some orphan with my face looking the way it did, and to top it off I was pregnant with no job.

I spent another few hours contemplating what I was going to do with the rest of my life. One thing was for sure, we would not be seeing Andrew ever again.

My first night in the B&B felt like being back in foster care in a way, by being told to live somewhere, that I had no say in and surrounded by strangers. I did, however, manage to adapt. I was getting good at that at least. I thought wryly.

I managed to get myself a cleaning job in a nursing home, which kept me busy during my out time from the B&B. I had also made several visits to a phone box to call my mother, to tell her the situation. She did seem genuinely concerned, and we met up a few times in a café.

Chapter Forty-Four

Stalked

I received a letter from the council offering me accommodation back on the chalet park on Lancing beach, where they had put me and my mother a few years before. Only it was just me, my mum was living with her boyfriend, and the council found out, and evicted me.

However, I was told that I would have to wait another four weeks.

Great! I thought sadly, but I had no options, for now, I had to stick with it.

∞∞∞

About three weeks later there was a knock on my room door. I expected it to be the lady of the house, as she was the only one that ever came to speak to me, but it wasn't. It was Andrew, all smiles and holding a bunch of flowers.

I let him in, as I was afraid to cause a scene and get kicked out, as that would not have been good for my housing application. Andrew sat himself down on my thinly covered double bed, which had more lumps than some badly mashed potato. I felt more than a little scared, and I really didn't want to be alone with him, and so I chose to not close the room door completely, which he noticed. I could tell it bothered him by the not so well hidden mask of irritation.

"I've got our house, the one we were going to look at." He said trying to sound cheerful.

Silence....

"I've also got a new car."

Silence.

"How did you know where I was?" I asked him quietly.

"I made a few calls. I also saw you at the café with your mother yesterday."

"You've been following me?" I asked apprehensively.

"I've been following you for over a week. You are carrying my child."

I felt like my blood was rushing from my body, and I was cold. I felt my knees tremble, and my heart was beating so loud, that I could hear it through my ears.

"You don't want my child Andrew. You made that quite clear." I spoke through trembling lips.

"Come on, I didn't mean what I said I was just in shock, and then I was mad because you were mad at me."

"With good reason." Dear God I couldn't handle this. I wanted him to leave. "Please leave Andrew."

"Leave you living like this with my child. No, come home, to our home. Our child can have a room of its own. There is a small garden."

"No Andrew I won't go back with you. You need help." I was afraid to say no, but I wasn't going back no way! I didn't want to raise a child in an abusive environment.

"You want him or her to grow up with a loving family don't you? and with a mother and a father. Isn't that what you always wanted a loving family? Please don't put our child through this. I want you, and I want our baby. I even want to get you an engagement ring. We could go shopping for one tomorrow."

Andrew tried holding me, and he began planting small soft kisses all over my face. I began to cry. I wanted so badly for him to change, to raise our child together, but not like this, not now, maybe not ever.

"It's not just my fault you know. It's you as well, with what you had to deal with as a kid, your too sensitive. Every couple fights, we just take it too far."

We… we take it too far? No, I didn't think so. It didn't take much of anything to set him off in a rage. It could be losing a bet on the horses, me talking to a man, any man, me not agreeing with something he said. I was the opposite I would do anything I could to avoid an argument.

A couple of years before, yes maybe I would have agreed. I was an angry person myself back then, but not now, now all I wanted was peace, to be happy.

I saw what he was doing. He was trying to manipulate me, take the blame from himself, and make me feel guilty. The only words that struck a chord with me were raising our child within a loving family with a mother and a father. He continued to kiss me, and he began to caress my belly, that was still quite flat.

"Look don't decide, let's go back to dating. We don't have to live together just yet. I will change, and when you feel you're ready, and then you can come home with me, where you and our baby belong. Our child will have loving grandparents, and plenty of aunts, uncles, cousins. That's what is best for our child. Let's just take it slow. What do you say? I don't want to lose you. I love you. Please just give me another chance?"

"I don't know," I responded. God, why couldn't I just tell him to piss off! I couldn't do it. I didn't agree with any of what he was suggesting, but I was just too damn afraid and he was right. I still cared for him, as I knew he could be wonderful when he wanted to be. I just couldn't trust him though. I did not feel safe.

∞∞∞

That evening he took me to a Chinese restaurant, and somehow managed to talk the landlady into letting him bring me back a bit later, so she wouldn't lock me out.

Then he managed to wangle his way into me letting him stay in the room with me, as he was too tired to drive back. I was too afraid to say no, and so I let him climb into bed and cuddle up to my stiff back. I barely slept at all, and I was stiff and sore from lying on one side all night. The last thing I wanted was to have to turn over and be face to face with him.

The next morning he woke me early with a cup of coffee using the kettle, and cups that were provided. I was always dubious about drinking the milk from the carton in the mornings, as there was no fridge in the room. I had to keep the milk in a small sink of cold water in the far corner of the room.

"I see you have a new place." He said waving the letter from the council in front of me. Damn, I must have left it out. I thought with dread.

∞∞∞

Andrew decided to spend the day with me, and I had to phone in sick at my new job. He bought me cheap engagement ring. Things like that never mattered to me. I would have been happy if it was a bit of tin foil wrapped around my finger. I say cheap because that's what he thought was best, just in case, things didn't turn out as he had planned, but at the same time, he wanted other people to know that I was engaged, and not single.

All I could do was smile wanly. Afterward, he drove me to the council office to see if I could get my keys early, and he waited in the car. They let me sign the housing agreement and collect the keys on the condition that I was happy to clean the place up myself, as it hadn't yet been done. I agreed and with the keys to the chalet I made my way back to Andrew.

Chapter Forty-Five

My New Shack

The chalets had really taken a nose dive in the last few years. The carpets were stained, as was the two seater sofa, with popped out springs. There were pen drawings all over the one bedroomed walls at the rear, and the mattress was covered in what looked like very old blood stains. I decided right then that I was going to sleep on the springy sofa, which turned out to actually be a sofa bed. The chalet was basically a caravan but made to look like a bungalow, with concrete steps leading up to the front and side doors.

Andrew looked utterly disgusted. I was too, but I didn't want to show it. Instead, I loaded up with cleaning supplies and fresh linens, further depleting my small savings. Andrew went back to Newhaven, leaving me to clean and fix the place up.

Nothing had changed around the site, it was still teeming with families, people getting high, drunk or into fights. Kid's ran rampant, some with no socks or shoes, some in nothing but their diapers, wandering freely away from their parents. It always worried me that they would be kidnapped or worse get hit by a moving car. I spent more time looking out for other people kid's from my window than I did trying to sort out my own mess of a home

It actually took several days for the carpets, and sofas to dry after my vigorous scrubbing of them. I ended up buying a blow-up bed to sleep on, in the small living area. I continued my cleaning job, and Andrew stayed with me most nights, and only driving to Newhaven for work. He made good on his word to try and change. The only problem was his constant complaining of my living situation, despite it only being temporary. In a way he was right, it was awful, but for me, it was all I had to cling to. It was my own.

∞∞∞

I was in my fourth month of pregnancy when I was invited to have dinner with Andrew and his parents at their home. Being there felt so familiar, the warmth, the sound of his mother in the kitchen, and seeing the big dining table laid out with cutlery and placemats, and everyone seated in their usual places.

"So Andrew has told me about where you are living." Said his mother, and she looked at me with sad eyes. "He misses you. We all do. Don't you think you would be better moving into a proper house with Andrew, for the sake of yourself, and our grandchild?" she said kindly.

"It's just temporary where I am. There should be news of a new flat or a house soon. Also, Andrew and I have agreed to take things slowly." I said rather timidly, but at the same time, I was trying to stay strong in my conviction.

"Families should be together. We all have our little arguments, but we don't go running off each time we have one. It's not fair Andrew driving back and forth every day from Lancing to work with his father and brothers. You two have a perfectly good house up the road, and in much better condition from what I hear."

"Mum, please let's not talk about this now. Evie is right, we need to take our time, and so far it's going great isn't it?" he asked looking at me with a smile and eyes full of hope.

Andrew's father was quiet, but he made several glances in my direction, and each time I smiled at him. God this was such an uncomfortable and awkward situation.

∞∞∞∞

After dinner, I helped his mother in the kitchen by drying the dishes, and she spoke to me of looking forward to seeing her grandchild. She made Andrew sound so sad, lost, and lonely without me being with him here, and that he was too good of a man to not try and rush me. I wondered if her husband had ever hit her? No, I didn't think so.

Where did Andrews's anger come from? Everyone else in his family who was married also seemed blissfully happy. What was wrong with us? Why couldn't we be as happy as them?

I had often tried to imagine what it would be like, living in the new house, our little family of three. I imagined the way the nursery would look, me cooking, and cleaning the house. All I wanted was to be in love, happy, and enjoy my pregnancy time with Andrew and going forth with our future. But when it came right down to it I was scared.

After I had helped his mother Andrew decided that it would be a good time for me to see the house, and so I reluctantly at first agreed.

∞∞∞∞

The red brick house with a blue door was at the top of a hill on a bend and situated between a row of other terraced houses. Next to the front door was a large bay window, with two other windows above it on the second floor.

Andrew opened up the front door, and directly in front of me was a flight of stairs, and the living room was on my right. There was a black, cast iron, Victorian fireplace, and two sofas. The kitchen was through a door to the left of the living room. It was oddly shaped, and slightly crooked looking at one end. There was also a back door, which I opened up to see a small triangular shaped garden with a long washing line, tied to a pole at the opposite end. On the top floor, there were three rooms, a bathroom, facing the back garden, a small double room beside it, and a large double room at the front of the house. Overall it was an old, but very nice house, unusually shaped, and it smelled quite musty, but it would make a very nice home.

"Well, what do you think?" Andrew asked me hopefully, with eyebrows raised.

"I think it's very nice. It needs more furniture and a good airing, but it's... nice."

"It needs you, and our child Evie." He said quietly, whilst looking at me.

"Is this why you brought me here Andrew, to make me change my mind?" I asked him cautiously, with a frown.

"No, well I thought it might help you, if you saw the place, maybe you could decide." He started to go into the next room whilst continuing. "I thought this room, next to the bathroom would make a wonderful nursery. What do you think?"

"I would like for you to take me home please Andrew if that's okay?"

I could tell he was clenching his teeth, behind his closed lips, as I could see his jaw tense, and the muscles in his cheeks twitching.

"Please. I'm sorry, I'm just feeling so good, and I'm tired. I do like the house Andrew, but I need to go home... to the chalet."

I spoke quietly as if I was trying to placate a small child, who was about to have a temper tantrum.

Andrew was quiet on the drive back to the chalet. I tried to make conversation a few times, but all I got in response was slight smiles or nods. I stayed alone that night, and I couldn't sleep. I ended up making a cup of coffee and sitting on the sofa, flicking between TV channels on the remote. Andrew was unhappy, and so far all he had done was try to make me happy. I was beginning to feel selfish. Was I being selfish not giving our child a decent home, and family around them? I was beginning to feel deeply sorry for Andrew. He was trying so hard and I was feeling that all he got from me was constant resistance. He wanted to live with his child and have them surrounded by family. I wanted that too.

Chapter Forty-Six

A family for a child

J ust over a month later I had finally agreed to move into our new house in Newhaven. The mortgage was three hundred pounds a month, it was manageable. I got another job working at the local Somerfield supermarket, as a checkout operator. My baby bump grew, and with it so did my love for our child. In my spare time, I spent time with Andrews's family. I read baby magazines, and played Lullaby music for the baby, to hear. I enjoyed long soaks in the bath, and watching my child move, sending ripples across my belly. I would caress my growing belly, as if I was hugging him or her, and trying to send as much love to them as I could, through my fingers.

Andrew would disappear off for hours at a time with his friend Simon, either going to the pub for a game of pool or taking him out to Brighton for the day. Simon had a brain tumor that was inoperable, and he suffered from seizures, and poor memory. Andrew was very good with him, Simon's parents and older brother were grateful that Andrew was helping their son to live a happy normal life as possible. I thought it was wonderful too, that he was being so caring and considerate.

∞∞∞∞

I had always kept in contact with my nan, and my father Peter, mostly by letter or the odd phone call. It was difficult to reach dad, as he would be out of the country most of the time, and it would take weeks for me to get a reply. He had sold the Lorry business, and opened an employment agency. It was then that he became a promotor for famous bands and singers. He invited me backstage to a few of their concerts over the years, and I got to meet boy zone, and the backstreet boys (who I confused the other with) it was very embarrassing. I wasn't really into pop music so I didn't really know who was who, or what they looked like. They thought it was pretty funny and forgave me. I met Ant and Dec, who were at the time P J & Duncan, singing "let's get ready to rumble". But after a while, he gave that up to and moved to Spain, and he became a part-time radio DJ.

My dad spent his time between Spain and the UK over the next few years. I never told my dad what was going on With Andrew. I would fill the letters with happy news, and questions about how he was, what he had been doing and such.

As luck would have it, he wrote to me saying that he was coming for a visit. I was super excited, though I had to book him into a B&B, just around the corner, as Andrew had been decorating the nursery, and already there was a cot and a chest of drawers, which I had been lovingly filling with tiny hats, mittens, and sleepsuits.

Chapter Forty-Seven

A New Baby

A few months later, some time after midnight, I awoke with a strange heavy feeling, and a desperate need to pee. As I sat on the toilet I felt a whoosh of Liquid. My waters had broken.

Mine and the baby's hospital bags had been packed ready and waiting a few weeks before-hand. I called the hospital, and I was told to stay at home, have a warm bath and wait for the contractions to get to five minutes apart, lasting a minute or so.

The pain was almost unbearable. I was hot, tired, and I couldn't keep still. I spent hours, and hours pacing around the bedroom, each time my belly contracted. I couldn't concentrate on anything but the pain. I clung to it, and nothing else.

When it was time to go to the hospital, I felt some hope of relief. I was placed in a good sized room with a large hospital bed and a see-through plastic crib in the corner of the room. My midwife was wonderful. Andrew sat in the high back chair beside my bed and he was busy calling his family on a new mobile phone that he had purchased. Mobile phones seemed to be all rage, personally, I didn't feel the need for one, but Andrew got me one too, a Nokia. I never used it.

The longer the labor progressed the more intense it got. I had managed pretty well up until a certain point, where I had gone from silently taking the pain, to loudly crying out. Andrew got annoyed with me for making so much noise, and at one point he voiced it by telling me "to just shut up with all that noise. Why do you have to be so loud?" just as the midwife was entering the room to check on me. The midwife gave him such a disgusted look and gave him a telling off. it didn't seem to bother him though, but he never said another word.

It got to the point where I became exhausted. I had been in labor for sixteen hours. The midwife asked me if I would like an epidural. I graciously and tiredly accepted.

"Thank god for that." I heard Andrew mutter. "You look awful." He muttered looking at me with something akin to disgust.

I never said anything. All I could do was sob quietly in the bed facing away from him.

At 7:26 pm our son Caleb was born, weighing 6lb 8 oz.'s. He was so small and peaceful swaddled up in a soft white blanket in my arms. Andrew had left shortly after Caleb was born, and I was glad. Andrew didn't hold him until he was cleaned and wrapped, and it was for only a few brief moments. I didn't mind, it meant that he was all mine to hold. I gently kissed his velvet soft cheeks and smiled at his little top lip which was formed in a small pink pucker. I stroked his smooth baby soft cheek with one finger and kissed the top of his silky dark hair.

"I love you so much little one. Welcome to the world little one. Happy birthday" I whispered, as I lay him down in the crib beside me.

When I awoke from a nap there was another lady across from me, and we exchanged pleasantries. Her husband was sitting beside her with his arm wrapped around her. They looked so happy, it was nice to see, but also quite painful watching them. I wished that Andrew and I could be like them.

The midwife had helped me get the hang of breastfeeding, as

I had chosen to give my newborn son my new milk for a few days, as apparently, it was very good for their immune systems. After a day or so I was discharged.

Chapter Forty-Eight

Wait till you get home

Andrew was spending more and more time away from home. If he wasn't working, he was with Simon, or at the betting shop. I had worked right up until the end of my pregnancy, and now I was on three-month maternity leave. I enjoyed waking up for the feeds, and nappy changes. I learned to get into a routine, which was to sleep when Caleb slept, and tackle everything else in between the feeding, changing, and bathing. I felt as if I was a single parent, lodging with someone who hated me, yet wanted me, but ... I found comfort in my son.

Andrew began beating me again when Caleb was around four month's old. If he was in a bad mood with someone or something, all I had to do was speak and it earned me a punch, kick, slap, or sometimes all three. I learned as time went on to try and keep myself busy, and to keep out of his way when he was in one of his moods.

Caleb was Six months old when Lucy came to visit. I was in the kitchen trying to pack clothes into the washing machine, and I accidentally trapped my thumb as I was closing the door. I exclaimed with a "shit!" and began sucking where my thumb had pinched.

Andrew who had been standing beside me at the sink without warning hit me around the back of the head so hard, it made my ears ring. As he hit me, my head bounced off the front of the washing machine. I didn't make a sound, and neither did Andrew. I was too afraid to alert Lucy because I knew Andrew would throw her out if she spoke, and I would probably get it much worse afterward. He had an intense dislike for my mother or anyone else from her side of the family, well everyone except Lucy. I didn't even look up at Andrew; I knew if I did then it would have earned me another slap. I gingerly rose and left the room to re-join Lucy in the living room. I painted on a bright smile as if everything was okay. Inside I was scared, but angry all at the same time. I was pathetic, weak, and useless.

∞∞∞∞

After my maternity leave was up I went back on the checkouts at Somerfield, but only for a few months. I managed to get myself a job as a night care assistant three nights a week. Andrews mum had agreed to look after Caleb for half days, so I could get some sleep after working the nightshifts.

I never tried to discuss with his parents or any of his other family members what was going on, though I knew his mother had an idea due to bruises on my face, arms and my stiffness sometimes, but she never asked, and I never told. What good would it do anyway? I used to think. Andrew would always wait until I had put Caleb down to sleep or physically remove me from a room so that our son couldn't see what he was doing. I was glad of that, at least.

∞∞∞∞

Andrew had decided one morning to take us out to Lewes for the day. Caleb was seventeen months old. There wasn't much really in Lewes at that time, a few clothes shops, and the Anne of Cleves house. The Anne of Cleaves really interested me, as I was very fond of history, and historical people. I knew that it was given to her by King Henry, but that she had never once stayed there. I had joined the library a few months before, and I have devoured several fiction and non fiction period books. Andrew wasn't really interested in any of that though.

I decided to ask Andrew if he wouldn't mind looking after our son, so I could have a look around the house, to which I was told "absolutely not!" and "why did I want to waste my time looking at shit that didn't matter anymore".

"Because I like it, and it's not shit! why are you being so miserable?!" I whispered crossly. That was a big mistake. He made me follow him back to the car, and forced me into the backseat, next to Caleb's car seat.

He started the car and made for home.

"Think you were clever? Well just wait till we get home, I'll bloody teach you!" he said darkly.

I looked up at him in the rear-view mirror. "I'm sorry I choked out. I didn't mean to say that. I know you're not miserable."

"You're just trying to be nice because you know what you're going to get." He spat back, like a venomous viper.

"No, that's not true. Please, Andrew. I'm sorry."

Chapter Forty-Nine

It was an accident

A ndrew made me sit down on the living room sofa, whilst he took Caleb up to his junior bed and closed his bedroom baby gate. I couldn't run, I wouldn't leave my son. I couldn't do anything, but sit, and wait for what was to come.

I couldn't breathe! He was wrapping a telephone cord around my neck, pulling and squeezing it. He would release it for a few seconds, so I could gasp for air and begin again. He did it two or three times. His face was fading in and out before me. I tried so hard to not pass out. My throat and head felt as if it was on fire, and my tongue felt swollen. He turned his back on me, whilst I was spread half on, and half off the sofa. I needed to move, I had to move. I dragged myself as fast as I could into the kitchen, and I shut the door, and slid down it, with my back to it. I could not leave this house; I would not leave my son, but what could I do?! I was screaming in my head.

Bang! Andrew began kicking the kitchen door, I assumed with his feet.

"NO! PLEASE ANDREW! I'm sorry, I'm sorry, I'm sorry." I shouted and cried at the same time.

The reverberation from him kicking the door went into my back, but I wasn't strong enough to hold the door. I was too weak, and he got in.

Evie Gallagher

∞∞∞

Andrew dragged me by my arm into the middle of the room, and then he grabbed my hair painfully and yanked me up until I was half standing. My legs were shaking. I couldn't hold my own body weight up.

I felt my head hit something hard. I don't remember falling after he let me go. I don't know what happened. I couldn't speak, and I couldn't move. I could hear Andrews voice in the next room, he was talking to someone.

"I think I've killed her. Mum please, come round." He was quiet, and then I heard the phone click. I kept my eyes closed. I must have bee knocked out I thought, or why else would he think I was dead? I thought. I didn't want to open my eyes. I couldn't take any more of a beating. Every cell in my body hurt, and my head was throbbing something terrible. I don't know how long I lay on the cold kitchen floor, it felt like hours. I heard a knock at the front door and the sound of his mother's voice.

"She's in the kitchen." I heard Andrew say.

I slowly opened my eyes, it would be safe for me to open my eyes, I hoped. I couldn't hear Caleb anywhere, and that worried me. I wondered where he was.

His mother entered the kitchen and gasped loudly.

"Andrew, what happened? What have you done to her?"

I looked up into her concerned face, as she tried getting me to sit up. The sharp pain in my head was so intense, and I felt something warm running down my neck. I put my hand towards it, and then I looked at my hand. It was covered in bright red blood.

Above me, on the white tiled wall was a circular, cracked dent. He must have shoved my head into the wall. I looked to the floor, and there were several small, tile shards on the lino by my feet.

"Can you get up?" she asked me.

"Y yes... I think so. Where is Caleb?" I asked fearfully.

"He's fast asleep in his bed." Replied Andrew rather quietly.

"We need to get you to a Doctor." His mother said aloud. "I'll take her. Come on up you get." She put her arms underneath my own from behind and tried pulling me up.

"I can do it. I I'll get up." I said shakily. I tried turning on my side, to get up onto my knees, and it hurt so much. It took me several attempts, but I finally managed, and pulled myself up, by using the cupboard and worktop as leverage. I leaned my weight forward on the worktop and tried feeling my head to see where the blood was coming from. It was coming from somewhere on the back, left of my head. It was too painful to touch. His mother grabbed some kitchen paper, wet it, and placed it on my head wound. It stung!

"What am I to tell the Doctor?" his mum asked worriedly.

"I don't know mum. We had a fight, it was an accident. I didn't mean to hurt her like that." He said in a frustrated tone.

His mother steered me by the arm towards the front door and helped me on with my coat, and together we made our way to the Doctor's surgery.

"If you say anything, they will take your child away from you, and Andrew would be very upset. You don't want to lose your son do you, Evie?"

"N no I don't want that." I sighed and I felt so incredibly tired. It was a struggle putting just one foot in front of the other. All I wanted to do was bury myself under a duvet and sleep. Sleeping was peace.

∞∞∞

I sat in the waiting room watching the large clock above the reception desk. I stared at the ticking hand, as it went past the twelve hands more than a dozen times. I felt Andrews mum fidgeting in her chair beside me, whilst making a few huffing noises every now and again.

A man called my name, and I looked up. That must be the Doctor then I thought, and I got up painfully from my chair. I felt Andrew's mum get up to, and I looked down at her.

"Don't worry, I'll go in. I'll be back in a moment." I said tiredly through slightly hooded eyes. She made to protest but I walked away.

I sat down in a hard orange plastic chair, and around the room at various certificates, and posters on flu jabs and asthma.

"Right what can I do for you?" he asked with a small smile.

"I had an accident... I fell and hit my head."

The doctor examined me and called in a nurse. The nurse cleaned my wound, which was not very long or deep, thankfully. The doctor placed some thin strip plasters across the wound and advised me to take painkillers. He checked my eyes, ears and blood pressure. My blood pressure was a little high, but he put that down to me being a young mother, and working nights. His advice was to try and get some more rest.

Chapter Fifty

Dangerous Deception

That night as I lay in bed I knew I had to leave Andrew, and take my son with me. Andrew was very careful with the remainder of the day, and evening. We each said very little. I busied myself playing with Caleb on the rug on the living room floor. I blew bubbles on his feet, and he would squeal in delight. I could feel Andrew's eyes on me all the while, studying me, trying to work out what I had told the Doctor because he was to chicken to ask me.

"I'm sorry." He muttered so quietly that I almost did not hear him.

I sat frozen, between not wanting to speak, and afraid not to respond in case he got upset with me again. My body couldn't take any more that day. My back felt bruised, along with my arms, my head, my neck, my face. I think the only thing that didn't hurt was the soles of my feet. I wanted to be strong. I wanted so badly to stand up, look him in the eye and tell him how much I hated him for what he had done that day, and many times before, but... I just couldn't do it. I was not brave enough, and I was weary. I felt hot tears roll down my cheeks, and I looked at my son, who was looking up at me with a beautiful, cheeky grin.

I gathered him up in my arms and took him upstairs for his evening bath, and then I tucked him in and read him a bedtime story. I stroked his soft wavy hair until he fell into a deep, peaceful slumber.

I had been lying in bed, right on the very edge in the dark, unable to fall asleep. I could hear Andrew's footsteps on the stairs, and so I painfully turned over onto my side facing the edge of the bed, and closed my eyes, pretending to be fast asleep. I could hear him undressing, and then climbing into bed. My body instantly tensed when I felt his arms wrap around my waist, ever so near my breasts... but I couldn't move. I could feel his cool breath on the nape of my neck, and I wanted to run. My body felt like a leaden weight, shutting down in fear.

"I know you're awake. I can tell by the sound of your breathing." He whispered brushing his lips against my ear. All I want you to do is forgive me. You make me so angry sometimes, and I lose control. I don't mean to hurt you. I want to love you." He said in a pathetic, whiny tone.

I could feel his work-roughened hands running from below my breasts to the top of my hip, over, and over again.

He took me that night, on the very same night that he thought he had killed me, and I lay there, eyes closed, and never made a single, solitary sound. When he was done he rolled over, pulling most of the duvet with him, and he fell fast asleep.

I turned back onto my side facing the edge of the bed. The top of my inner thighs sticky, and my quiet sobbing gently shook the bed. If Andrew ever realized, then he never spoke a word, and I never slept, and never moved.

∞∞∞

The next morning before Caleb had awoken I got in the bath. The water was almost scalding hot, as I had barely put any cold in. I scrubbed every inch of my body, and very gingerly I washed my hair. I wasn't supposed to but I did. When I got out I covered myself in moisturizer and dressed. I then went down to the kitchen, made myself a cup of coffee, and began making Andrews lunch for work.

By the time he had come down unshaven, wearing paint, and cement stained jeans and a white t-shirt in the same condition, I was already in the process of giving Caleb his morning breakfast.

"Good morning." I greeted him happily and smiling at him as lovingly as I could manage. He looked at me a little surprised, and he nodded in greeting.

"I've made you a nice lunch, it's in your box, in the fridge," I said, smiling, whilst trying to encourage Caleb to eat his apple porridge, by pretending his dripping spoon was an airplane.

"Thanks. I um, I'm heading out to Seaford today, there's a new job Dad, and I are going to look at." He said trying to sound as cheerful as I was I thought.

"Oh, that's great! Well little man and I are heading off to the park to feed some ducks I said to Caleb playfully, but I was actually telling Andrew. Afterward, I thought I would get some shopping, and take Caleb to see the girls at Somerfield, and then maybe cook us all a nice roast. What do you think?" I asked with raised brows and a smile."

I was overdoing it I thought alarmingly over and over. I needed to relax, not sound so eager, and happy. I was sure by the look on his face that he was going to ask me what I was up to, but he didn't.

"That sounds good. I'll look forward to it." He smiled.

He's either playing me, or he's buying into my charade. I hoped he believed me. I wasn't usually this eager or smiley with him. But then his smile dropped, and he walked over to me. I felt myself backing up to the kitchen worktop, and he placed a hand either side of me. His face was mere inches away from my own. Dear god, he knows I'm up to something. My body stiffened, and I was holding my breath. I did not realize that I was until I the needed to take a breath in. He took the pretend airplane teaspoon out of my hand, placing it beside me on the worktop, and he continued looking at me dead center.

"I know what you're up to." He said slowly in a deeper sounding voice.

"I I'm n not up to anything Andrew." I stuttered my words as I began to speak, but I tried to smile.

"Yes... you... are." He spoke slowly, separating his words teasingly.

"You're trying to make up for yesterday, aren't you?" he asked me, now looking a little more serious, but he was almost panther-like in his demeanor.

I couldn't believe he thought I had anything to make up for! I didn't beat him up or smash his head off a wall, and then try to make have sex! No, I didn't believe he really thought that. He was trying to lessen his own guilt, and onto me, as was his custom. I felt sick. God, I had to think of something to say and make it good.

"Well, I shouldn't have snapped at you in Lewes yesterday. I should have treated you with more respect. I'm sorry Andrew. I do want to make things better between us. I don't like it when we fight." I couldn't look at him when I spoke, and so I said it looking down at the small gap between us. Caleb was beginning to get fidgety in his highchair, and he was trying to wriggle free of the waist strap. Andrew was distracted by that, and he smiled at his son. He picked him up and held him next to us.

"I am too. You know that I love you both, and I'm sorry as well for... taking it too far. I don't mean to hurt you, you know?" he said almost sincerely, as he continued to study my face.

"I know." I gave him a small peck on the cheek and held my arms out for our son. "I had better get this little one cleaned up, and ready to go and feed these ducks." I made my voice sound as bright an airy as I could, even though all I wanted to do was tell him that I was leaving and that he would never see us again. Instead, I smiled, as I took Caleb in my arms, and walked as calmly as I could away from the kitchen... and Andrew.

"Well, I'll say goodbye now then. I will try to get home earlier." He called cheerfully after us.

"Yes okay. We will see you later."

Chapter Fifty-One

Running for my life

I nervously waited for Andrew to leave for work. When I heard the front door shut I listened anxiously for his van to start. I walked to the bedroom window, peering through the thin lace curtain, watching him driving off.

I immediately grabbed two holdalls, one for me, and one for Caleb, and I began going from each of our rooms stuffing as many clothes as I could into them. I then placed a bag strap over each shoulder. I then scooped Caleb up and very carefully went downstairs.

I placed Caleb on the living room rug, letting the holdalls slip off my shoulders. As quickly as I could I grabbed a carrier bag and filled it with his juice cups, and then I got several nappies, from the cupboard under the stairs.

I was about to pick up the holdalls when I heard the familiar sound of a van out the front of the house. I stopped frozen, holding my breath to hear better. I then heard the slam of a van door, and it was then that I released my breath in a whoosh. I picked Caleb up off the floor, just as I heard the key in the lock of the front door.

There was no time to grab the bags, and so I ran opening the back door, and I took off running up the garden path. I went out through the gate, turned right, and ran down a short gravel road. I almost stumbled in a blind panic, and I felt something cut my feet through my socks. I had no shoes, no coat, no bags, and no money. Caleb was wearing a little jogging outfit, and he had no shoes or coat either. It wasn't a particularly cold in the month of March, but I didn't have time to think. I had to run as if I was running for my life because if he caught me I didn't think I would live another day.

I could hear Andrew yelling my name, he wasn't far behind, but I didn't dare look back. I had to keep going and not stop!. I was running as fast as I could trying to support my child cradled on my hip, with both arms wrapped around him, and I was starting to lose my breath. I felt as if he was right on my heels, and so I tried to run faster. Caleb was bobbing up and down furiously on my hip, and my arms began to feel the strain of his weight, despite the fact that he wasn't really a heavy child at all. I could hear a whistling sound in my throat, and it was getting harder, and harder to get more air into my lungs, but I just could not stop. I rounded a corner, which brought me out onto the main road, and a few yards ahead there was a bus. I began waving one of my arms furiously, and I shouted Wait! Please! Using up what felt like the last of my oxygen.

I made it, just as the bus doors were about to close.

"Please, I begged the driver breathlessness. Please drive." The older bus driver looked perplexed, but thankfully he closed the doors. As he did Andrew slammed his fists against the bus door as it had closed.

"Don't let him on!" yelled a female passenger.

"Please drive." I panted, trying so hard to catch my breath, after which Caleb began to cry. I rubbed his back, and took myself to the nearest seat and sat down with him on my lap.

The driver began to drive off, leaving Andrew behind. A lady had come to sit beside me, and as soon as she spoke I recognized her as the one who yelled to the driver to not let Andrew get on the bus.

"You look like a deer caught in headlights love. Are you and the little fella alright?" she asked with a frown and a face full of concern.

"Yes, I think so. I need to get to Brighton, but I'm afraid he will follow the bus" I said shakily.

The lady got up and went to the bus driver's window, and then she came back after several seconds.

"Now don't you worry I've spoken to the driver, when we get off at the town bus station, we are going to escort you onto the Brighton bus. Do you want me to call the police? She asked talking a mobile phone out of her handbag.

"No, no police. Thank you. I just need to get on the other bus. I responded, but instead of looking at her I was anxiously staring out of the window, to try and see if Andrew was following behind in his van, but I couldn't see.

A few minutes later the bus pulled up at the last stop, behind the town center shops. The driver opened his door and asked everyone to stay on the bus for a moment, whilst he spoke to another driver. I could hear the other passengers, a dozen or so murmuring amongst themselves, however, they complied without complaint.

The driver emerged after a couple of minutes and ushered myself and Caleb off the bus, onto another one just in front.

"Thank you." I said, "Thank you." I looked and saw the lady passenger behind the driver, and she smiled to wave me off. The new driver closed the doors. He was older than the other one, but he looked warmly at me.

"Please, can you take me to Brighton? I don't have any money, but I promise you that somehow I will get the money to you for the fare." I pleaded quickly and rather desperately.

"There's no need for that love. Take a seat. I'll get you to Brighton. Where in Brighton do you need to go?" he asked.

"I'm actually going to Lancing, but I have to get a different one from Brighton, so maybe somewhere in Brighton city center?" I spoke quickly, just anxious for the bus to get moving. I felt that Andrew was close by ready to drag me off the bus. I think the driver sensed my anxiety for he asked me to take a seat directly behind him and told me we could talk on the way.

There was only a couple of older teenage kid's on this bus, and they were seated right at the back, thankfully more interested in their own conversation.

When the bus had pulled out and made the turning for Brighton I began to relax a little.

"Listen. I will talk to one of the drivers and get you a ticket for Lancing. Don't worry about the money; it's on me, including this fare."

"Thank you, thank you so much. I promise I will pay you back." I responded in grateful relief.

The driver and I chatted most of the way. He was a lovely man, who was married, with two older daughters, and three grandchildren. He didn't ask me why I was in this situation, but I figured the last driver had told him about Andrew banging on the bus looking madder, then even I had seen him the day before.

Chapter fifty-two

Drained

I walked from Lancing village, all the way with Caleb on my hip to mum, and Derek's house. My mum had gotten back with Derek not long after Caleb was born. It was this house I chose, as I had nowhere else to go. I got plenty of funny looks. I knew of course why they were staring. There was a young woman with a small child, no pram, no coat, and no shoes. I was embarrassed, and I just wanted to get to the house as quickly as possible.

Derek said very little to me, but my mother was all action and for that I was grateful. She helped me get Caleb settled with some juice, and some lunch, whilst digging out some of my old clothes and shoes. The shoes were okay, but the clothes felt quite tight. I hadn't gained that much weight had I?

My mother had one of my aunties take me to the council offices, and then onto the jobcentre to sign on for single parents, and they gave me thirty pounds cash in hand, which I had to sign for as a put me on until a few days time. I felt so ashamed. I wanted better than this for my child, for myself. But needs must, there was no other option I couldn't rely on mum to feed us both.

I was placed once more into the Chalets next to Lancing beach, and mum took me to the charity shop to get some clothes for Caleb, and me. We then bought some food to last us a few days, and my mother gave me some spare bedding.

∞∞∞

We didn't have much Caleb and me, but I was safe, and he was with me, and that's all that mattered. I gradually managed to replace borrowed things for things of our own such as small electrical appliances, crockery, and furnishings. I started taking Caleb to a drop in playgroup a few times a week to toddle about with some other kids his age, and I enjoyed chatting with other mums. I devoted everything I had to my son, he was...my everything. I wanted him to have a wonderful and happy upbringing. I learned to make him play-doh, we went to the park every day, and I made us small picnics and we would sit on the beach eating ice-cream. I took him swimming on Sundays. The only thing I needed to do now was to find myself a job, but in doing that I would need to find a sitter, and I wasn't ready to trust anyone with my son, not after what I went through as a small child. I couldn't risk leaving him with a stranger. My mother now worked full time in a nursing home, and therefore she was now only drinking in the evenings.

I began waking up with the ever familiar morning sickness. I didn't need to do a test I knew I was pregnant. I went to the Doctor anyway and I had it confirmed.

"Well, little one. It looks as though you are going to be a big brother, lucky you." I said to him, kissing his soft cheek.

I couldn't cry. I couldn't even be angry. There was another tiny life already taking root within my body, and I would love this child like I loved my son. Everything was going to be okay.

Another month went by and one of my aunts came to visit me at the chalet. It seemed that Andrew and his mother had been calling around everyone trying to find out where I was. I wasn't really surprised, though I was surprised that he hadn't found me already. Thankfully my aunt hadn't told him anything, and she gave Andrew's mum a piece of her mind. My mother and Derek never said a word either.

I carried on my usual routine of taking Caleb to playgroups, the park, and to the beach for picnics. After a few more months my belly grew larger and more rounded. I was still sick though, not just in the mornings but throughout the days and sometimes at night too. I began to feel more tired than I was when I was pregnant the first time, and I took to having short naps during the day with Caleb. Despite my gaining a pregnancy tummy I had lost a lot of weight everywhere else. I made sure to drink and eat as much as I possibly could, and I kept all my regular appointments.

∞∞∞∞

When I was into my seventh month of pregnancy I still felt no better. I had gotten thinner, everywhere except for my ever expanding belly. My face was pale, and dark circles had formed around my eyes. I felt tired and weak almost all the time. Caleb was a busy toddler, always on the go. I managed to keep up with him until I had put him down to sleep. I used to worry that once my head hit the pillow I would be out light a light, and not be able to wake if Caleb woke up. Thankfully though... I always stirred. I had to stop taking him to the beach after a while as the weather was turning colder, and the park was now too far to walk. I was forced to swap fun and fresh air for Bob the builder Video's, and baking cupcakes. When it wasn't raining I would sit out on a chair and watch him ride about in his little red and yellow car outside the chalet.

I had bought a crib, and some second-hand baby clothes and I had been stockpiling milk as well as nappies for a few months. Our neat little chalet was getting to be quite cramped, but I knew that when the new baby was here I would need everything.

Quite often Caleb would lay his head on my tummy, or rub my belly to bring comfort to his new baby brother or sister. He used to snatch his little hand away from my tummy and giggle when he could feel the kicks.

Chapter Fifty-Three

Helpless

I had filled Caleb's bath with bubbles. The bath was quite literally overflowing with white foam, and there were suds covering parts of the bathroom floor. Caleb stood up in the bath holding onto a large foamy cloud, he was trying so hard to blow away the foam, as I had done making the suds blow up into the air. I laughed watching him, as he giggled in his foamy delight.

I heard a knock at the door. "Give me just a minute!" I called out. "That must be your Grandma," I said smiling. "Be a good boy now and don't move till you see me," I told him in careful warning.

Thankfully the bathroom was right beside the front door, so I only had to lean around to open it.

"Andrew!" I exclaimed. Immediately I felt fear as well as dread. I was going to be sick. I put my arm protectively over my belly, and I tried to close the door in his face. It was no good. Andrew was much stronger than me, and he invited himself in. I drew back blocking the bathroom door. I glanced back at Caleb who was still happily splashing. I quickly decided to let the plug out, and I told Caleb that when the water was gone, it was time to get out.

I turned back around to Face Andrew who was now sat on the sofa in the living room. I glanced around furiously looking for my mobile phone. It was right on the arm of the sofa beside him. My glance didn't go unnoticed, and Andrew picked up my phone and played with it in his hands.

"Andrew you need to leave, please. Now is not a good time." I pleaded, my voice shaking.

"I've missed you both, and I see we have another on the way." He said lightly, whilst nodding in the direction of my swollen belly.

"Andrew I don't want any trouble. Please, can you come back tomorrow?" I asked, glancing again behind me at Caleb who was still messing about with the bubbles. "I need to get Caleb dried and ready for bed."

"Carry on. I would like to say goodnight to him too." He smiled.

He wasn't going anywhere, and I knew it. I had no way of getting help. I had no choice but to let him stay. I wouldn't dare try and make a run for help after Caleb was in bed. I wouldn't leave my son.

I deftly lifted him out, suds and all, wrapped him up in his soft fluffy towel and placed him a few feet from the electric heater. Sure that he would be warm enough, I removed his towel and dried him off. He began to giggle when I began to dry his hair, and he tried reaching for the baby powder on a small table beside him. All the while I could feel Andrew's eyes on us both from behind me. Normally I would be enjoying Caleb's evening bath, and story time ritual, but not tonight. I was once again met with the same awful feeling of dread, as I had done once before. I was on constant alert, my body stiff, and unrelaxing. I had enjoyed these last few months of not feeling my stomach in constant knots when he was around.

Andrew urged Caleb to come to him, once I had powdered and dressed him in his little blue pajamas. Caleb went to him, and clumsily, tried to kiss him goodnight.

I read to Caleb a story and stayed with him until he had fallen asleep, with his arms wrapped around his small brown bear, and his bottom lip stuck out in a small pout. I did something that I didn't usually do – I closed his bedroom door completely. I walked through the small galley kitchen and tried steeling myself for the unknown.

When I returned Andrew was still seated on the badly faded beige sofa, which I had tried to cover up with a second-hand blanket, not quite big enough. There was powder on the brown carpet in front of the heater, and there were building blocks scattered in a small corner. I began collecting up the blocks, putting them back in his toy box, and then I went to the bathroom to turn off the light. I wanted to keep busy, but I knew that I was only delaying the inevitable, and so did he.

I waited, standing in front of him silent, unmoving, waiting for his anger, and berating, but it never came, instead, he put his head between his knees... and cried.

I felt confused and unsure, torn between asking him what was wrong and asking him to leave us alone. I felt like all the courage and self-reliance that I had built up since leaving foster care, until the time that I had met Andrew was gone. I was a pathetic, scared little mouse with no idea how to get myself out of this situation.

There was nothing left in me to try and fight. I was too scared to stand up and tell him to leave. In my mind, I knew that if I were to, then I would risk the life of the child I carried, and so I did all I knew how to at this point – I kneeled down in front of him, and I gave in, silently crying.

Chapter Fifty-Four

Broken in spirit

In the months that Caleb and I had been gone, Andrew had sold the house in Newhaven, bought himself another new car, and moved into a row of flats above a shopping center in Peacehaven. The entrance was to the rear of the shopping center. There was a heavy door with several different call buttons on a panel beside it. Once you managed to get through the door there were two flights of concrete stairs, and another heavy door when you got to the top. I followed a bricked balcony wall off to the left, and walked past two other flat doors on my right, before getting to ours on the end. Our balcony overlooked a small, green playing field, and to the left of the field was a small community center.

We had a small roof garden and beyond the wall was the expansive flat roof, of the shopping center. There were several large air conditioning units which hummed constantly day and night. The garden was covered in large patio tiles on one side, and grey shale on the other.

Our caretaker was a man called Bob. He would often sit in his cramped little office, attached to a row of garages, across the car park from the flats. Bob was quite a chatty fellow, though I did find him slightly strange, I don't know why – I just did.

I brightened up the garden with colorful pots, and I planted lots of brightley colored flowers to brighten it up a bit.

I re-registered Caleb, and I at a small doctor's surgery to the left of the carpark. The surgery was on a grassy island, surrounded by neat shrubs. The doctor gave me something for the sickness, and Andrews mum visited most days to help me catch up on some sleep, and she also helped with the housework. Sometimes we would often walk to the children's play park, and take turns pushing him in the baby swing. Andrews mum was a wonderful Nan to the kid's; she lived for all of her children, as well as grandchildren. Nothing was ever too big or too small for her where they were concerned. His mother had let me know on a few occasions that I was wrong for leaving the way I did and taking Andrew's son away. All I could do was agree, and promise that I wouldn't do it again, and after a while she forgave me.

I decided after a couple of months before my due date to enroll Caleb at playgroup in the small community center three times a week. I would take him in at 9 am and collect him at lunchtime. Caleb really enjoyed it, and it gave me a few precious hours of alone time. I would quite often have a nosey around the shopping center, or sit and read a whole bunch of historical novels. My favorite one was about a lady going back in time through a stone circle, and falling in love with an Elizabethan earl. I also loved to read the prophecies of Nostradamus, and books about palm reading. The latter books led me to read other books about spirituality, healing with Reiki, and how to meditate – I was fascinated by them.

∞∞∞

Late one afternoon I got a call from my dad. He was back in

the UK for a few days and wanted to visit. I was always excited to see my Dad and finding out what he had been up to. He had bought himself a motorbike, and he had been traveling around Europe. He always bought something back for Caleb on his adventures, and this visit was no different.

Dad as usual booked himself into a bed and breakfast for a couple of nights, and so after a cuppa, I walked him down with Caleb in my arms, so he could drop off his bags, and freshen up for a planned meal later on.

My dad knew about what had been happening. He was upset that I went back to Andrew, but I begged him to please not say anything for my sake. He agreed. It was very difficult for him though, but I was grateful.

As I kissed my dad on this cheek and waved goodbye a white piece of paper flapping in the light breeze caught my eye. The paper was pinned down underneath the window wiper on Andrews's car. Curiously I pulled it free to read what was written in black ink.

Andrew I can't see you anymore,

Please don't contact me anymore

M.

I felt my stomach drop. Who was M? And how long had they been seeing each other? I felt bile rise up in the back of my throat, and I had to dash with Caleb in my arms back up the two flights of stairs, trying desperately to reach the flat before I threw up. I had just managed to put him down before I emptied what little contents there was in my stomach. I wretched over and over despite nothing really coming out yellow bile. My face was burning hot, and fat tears streamed down my cheeks from my heaving. I looked at Caleb who had toddled his way to the bathroom door and was staring at me with a look of deep concern.

I placed a cool damp cloth on my face to cool it down. I then scrubbed my mouth with my toothbrush and some minted toothpaste.

I never once questioned Andrew about the note I found. After I had freshened myself up I went down to the car and put the note back where I had found it.

I barely ate my meal with Andrew, my dad, and Caleb that night. I spoke mechanically, pasting what was probably a very unrealistic smile on my face, at moments throughout my dad and Andrews conversations, where I felt it was appropriate. I was unable to really focus on the exact topics of what they were discussing, and I took my cues from their animated faces more than anything.

By the end of the evening, Dad hugged me goodbye and promised to be back the following morning, after his morning breakfast at the B&B.

Andrew announced that he was going out with Simon for a few drinks, and he left me to, with barely a backward glance.

I spent the remainder of the evening cleaning washing the dishes and putting the dinner table back to rights. Once that was done I set about bathing Caleb, and then getting him settled in bed. I lay down beside him, and I put on a Bob the builder video, his favorite. I had lost count the number of times I had watched it with him, but I didn't mind, and he always fell asleep about halfway through.

When I woke up I was still beside him, and he was sleeping peacefully with his little arm around my neck. My back was stiff, and I could feel the baby kicking my ribs. I assumed that and my back is what woke me. I gently with effort managed to slide myself off the end of his bed, and then I quietly crept out.

I popped my head into the other room. The bed was still made, and Andrew had not come home yet. I didn't bother with pajamas, I knew I would be up again in a few short hours, and so I ran myself a warm bath and slid myself into the water, the bubbles enveloping me... and I cried. I cried as quietly as I could feel as if my heart was breaking. My chest felt heavy like there were unseen hands tugging at my heart and chest. I didn't want to be alive anymore. I wanted to slide myself down into the water, and not come back up. But I couldn't do it. I had Caleb to think of and another child still growing in my belly. I just could not do it. I cried for a long time until the water had grown considerably cooler. I got out, dried myself off, and put on my dressing gown feeling some-what dead inside.

I heard the front door open and then close. I sat down on the toilet lid and waited in the locked bathroom until he had gone to bed. I quietly crept out and lay down on the sofa, caressing my swollen belly.

When I opened my eyes it was light, and I could hear Caleb chattering away in his room. I got up as quickly as I could to check on him. I opened the baby gate and scooped him up into my arms. He looked like he had not long awakened, and he was smiling at me so beautifully. I kissed his little cheeks, then set him down on his bed, I popped another of his cartoon video's in the VCR, and then switched his TV back on.

"Now I'll be back in a minute darling. I will make you some breakfast, and we can sit at the dining table okay?" I said to him with a soft smile.

Closing the gate behind me I noticed the time on the clock, and my dad was due in the next thirty minutes. I decided to wake Andrew, to see if he was able to help me with Caleb, whilst I sorted our breakfasts. When I entered the room Andrew was bundled deep in the duvet, and all I could see was his sandy brown head pocking out the top.

"Andrew, you need to wake up, my Dad will be here soon and we have all slept in." I got no response. I was really unsure about trying to wake him, but I didn't have much choice as we had made plans to all meet up with his parents. I gingerly reached out my hand and touched where I guessed his shoulder was, and give him a small shake.

"piss off" he snapped from under the covers.

"Andrew I'm sorry, but my dad will be here soon, and I need help with Caleb."

"I said... PISS OFF!" he roared at me, thrusting back the bed cover. He looked wide-eyed at me, his hair all flattened on one side of his head.

"Didn't you hear me? He said darkly."

I could feel my knees beginning to shake. I wanted to move but my body felt like a leaden weight. I needed to get dressed, but he was ordering me out of the room. What was I to do?"

"Okay. I'm sorry Andrew I I just need to get some clothes." I was tightly clutching the lapels of my dressing gown together. I decided to move quickly, and get some clean clothes, and dress in the bathroom. But before I knew what was happing he lashed out with his foot kicking me hard in the stomach. I didn't have time to react, to think, because In the next instance I was being pinned down on top of the bed. Andrew was holding both of my arms above my head, and he had straddled me, with a leg either side of me, and he rested himself below my bulging stomach. He was shouting at me. I could see was this rage, teeth, and his eyes. His eyes looked so much darker, wider. He then began choking me with his bare hands, so tight... I couldn't breathe. I could feel spittle on my chin, and just as I was sure I was going to die from asphyxiation, he released his grip on my neck. I breathed in deeply, trying to take as many precious deep breaths as I could. I began coughing and as I did I spat.

"Trying to spit at me were you?" he yelled at me red-faced, eyes still bulging. "I'll show you spitting."

Over and over he spat in my face his face just inches from my own. I had to close my eyes when I could feel the runny globs going in them. I tried to close my mouth too, but I couldn't I just kept on gasping for air. He would stop for several seconds getting his breath, and more spit, and began once again to spit in my face, my hair, my neck.

Eventually, he released my numb, powerless arms and climbed off me. I lay there frozen in fear, covered in his spit, and my dressing gown had come open, baring my breasts, and my bump, where I hoped my child would still be okay. It was the thought of my child that snapped me back to a sort of reality. I slowly sat up. Andrew was pacing the room back and forth between getting his jeans, and fresh underwear from the drawers. I could hear Caleb's cartoon playing in the background, and I could hear him babbling away to himself. Andrew never once looked at me or spoke to me. Whilst he dressed or when leaving the room.

I walked over to the mirror stand at the end of the room. My hair was damp around my pallid face, and I could see his disgusting spit all over my face, and neck. My neck was red and sore. I knew that if I tried to speak my throat would be so dry that I would barely be able to speak. I continued to stare at myself and I remember not being able to feel, I couldn't cry, there was just nothing, no emotion whatsoever.

Mechanically I cleaned myself up, and I got dressed and wrapped a scarf around my neck to hide the marks. I didn't feel my baby move till much later on in the evening. I was much too scared to ask Andrew to go to the hospital, and in truth, I was afraid that they were going to tell me that my child was gone, because he kicked me so, painfully hard.

Chapter fifty-five.

A mothers love for her children

On a cold December morning, our daughter Holly was born on the way to the hospital, in the back of an ambulance, at 3:42 am. She was so quiet. I expected her to cry at the injustice of having to leave her warm haven, where she had been growing for the past nine months. Instead, she just looked at me, silently, and peacefully scanning my face.

"Hello baby, aren't you precious? I love you. Happy birthday, beautiful girl." One of the ambulance men who had held my hand throughout the journey, due to a home birth gone wrong because I threw up, and my midwife was jittery with me being her first ever home birth patient. I actually ended up beginning the pushes as I was being helped into the waiting ambulance. He wished me well and thanked me for letting him stay to be present at his first ever childbirth. Andrew arrived shortly after they had settled Holly and me onto the maternity ward. He had taken Caleb to his parent's house and brought me my bags. I watched as he picked up our daughter, in much the same way he did with our son... with love in his eyes, and a smile on his face. It was painful watching him the way he was with his family, his nieces and nephews. Even watching him with his now two children. Why was it so hard for him to look at me that way, with love. Why couldn't he smile at me, or laugh with me, instead of at me? I had said to him once that if he didn't love me, then he should just let me go. My answer was simple...

"Because you are not taking my kid's away from me." He said coldly.

When Holly was ten days old she was rushed into hospital with acute bronchiolitis. She was taken to intensive care and placed inside a large incubator with holes in the sides. The nurse had to insert tubing through her nose to suck out excess fluid that kept trying to fill her tiny lungs. The next day the Doctor ordered her to be put on a CPAP machine to take over her breathing, so she could rest. Her little tiny body was so tired from trying to fight off the bronchiolitis. The nurse gave me a key to a house that was used by other parents, with seriously ill children. It was called the Ronald McDonald house. But I didn't take it. I was not going to leave my daughter's side. I sat for almost two days straight in a chair beside her incubator, stroking her small velvet soft hand. The only time I left was to use the toilet. By that second day, I began to feel very ill, and my breasts were incredibly hot, and painful.

One of the nurses contacted a midwife and asked her to pop in and see me. It turned out that I had got mastitis in both of my breasts. I hadn't been able to breastfeed, and I hadn't been able to pump. But still, I wouldn't leave her side.

The nurse that contacted the midwife had arranged for a porter to wheel me in a guest bed, and they put it in place of the chair. I caught the nurse having a little cry behind the nurses' station I managed to get myself up and, I gave her a gentle hug, all I could say was... Thank you.

Andrew still had to work, and his parents were caring for Caleb, but every evening for visiting Andrew would come along, and bring him along. I missed my little boy so much. I was worried that he would be feeling confused, and left out, but he seemed quite happy. I cried each time Andrew took him home. I felt selfish, but I just couldn't leave our daughter in this place without anyone beside her. I just could not do it.

∞∞∞

Holly was transferred from intensive care to the baby ward after eight days. Only when she was out of danger and starting to get better did I consider using the key to the Ronald McDonald house to freshen up, and eat quick microwave meals. There was a bedroom, but I still wouldn't sleep so far away from her. I continued my naps in a high back chair in her windowed room, Surrounded by beeping machines.

∞∞∞

I had to say that out of everything that had ever happened to me thus far, was by the scariest time of my life. I would have lived every single terrible thing that had ever happened to me again if it meant that my daughter would live. It was the first time in my life that I had prayed. I would have given anything to see my daughter healthy and happy, instead of so tiny, sick and utterly helpless.

∞∞∞

By the tenth day in the hospital, she was well enough to be discharged. I couldn't thank the hospital staff enough. They were so wonderful, caring and very professional.

Caleb enjoyed having his new sister back home again, and he

was very cuddly with me over the next few days. I had missed him so much, and I was just relieved to be home in the company of both my children.

I continued taking Caleb to morning nursery school, which he absolutely loved. I was asked to help them out on the odd mornings when they were short staffed. I happily agreed, and I would sometimes stay to hand out the mid-morning juice, and a fruit snack. Other days I would help with activities, such as arts, and crafts or minding the soft play, or even face painting. I enjoyed it, as I got to see how my little boy was getting along and have Holly with me too. It was nice being out of the flat and in happy surroundings.

I did find it difficult to make new friends, as I had grown very nervous, and shy. I would be happier listening to the conversations that the other mums were having as opposed to joining in. I remember feeling very awkward, and a little uncomfortable, when they asked me questions about Andrew or our family life. I guess I was a little scared at getting too friendly, as that meant I would have to invite them round for a cuppa, and long chats. And what could I say? What could or couldn't I tell them? Ohh I'm sorry I can't invite you round because the father of my children beats me, and speaks to me like I'm the dirt beneath his shoes. Maybe if I told them that then they wouldn't want to speak to me because it would be too embarrassing for them, or maybe they just wouldn't want their children to associate with mine.

On the days that I wasn't helping at the nursery I would get the bus to see Andrew's mum or I would be out walking with the pram, but more often than not I was in the library. I enjoyed the quiet, I was not alone and I didn't need to interact with anyone. It was perfect.

Chapter Fifty-Six

Mother's Day

It was mother's day and Holly was only three months old. Caleb had made me a card at nursery, and so I already had it displayed proudly on the wall unit in the living room.

Andrew was home, and he had dressed and fed Caleb, whilst I bathed Holly and got her ready in a pretty pink frilly dress with a matching headband.

Afterward, I popped her in her bouncing chair in front of the cartoons. Caleb then sat down beside her, trying to give her his teddy bear. I smiled, loving how thoughtful he was. I went to the kitchen to fix us some breakfast, and I warmed a bottle for Holly.

Andrew disappeared off for about half an hour, I didn't know where, but when he came back he was in a foul temper. Whenever he was like this I would take the children out, and come back when I deemed it safe enough and I planned to do exactly that, as soon as I had fed them but... it wasn't to be.

His presence moving around me in the kitchen made my body stiffen. I was buttering a slice of toast, though I didn't think that I would be able to swallow it.

BANG! He slammed an overhead cupboard door beside me, making me startle, and jump.

"Get out of the bloody way!" he shouted, almost in my ear. I could feel his breath on the side of my face. I remember thinking oh god, oh god, and I moved, leaving my partially buttered slice of toast.

"Look at this mess! Aren't you going to clean it up?" he snapped at me.

I couldn't look at him, afraid that it would make it worse, and so I bowed my head a little, brushing off the crumbs on my fingers.

"I am going to clean it after I have fed the children. I'm sorry." My voice had betrayed me, for my words were only a mere whisper.

"You're pathetic." He said flatly "why can't you keep everything clean?" he spat out.

I looked around the kitchen; there were the crumbs from the toaster on the worktop, two plates, and a can of baby formula out from the bottle making. There were a few cups in the sink, and that was about it, and a pan on the drainer. I was always very careful to make sure everything was always clean and tidy. I was more of a do what you need to do, then clean up afterward, instead of cleaning as you go along, sort of person. Andrew had never really complained before, he knew it would be tidied, as soon as I could. That was always the way. But I couldn't argue back. There was nothing I could say, without making him worse. My punishment was coming, I could feel it, and there was nothing I could do or say that would stop it.

I felt the full force of his flat hand as he slapped my head; half of his hand caught my cheek, and I could hear my ear ringing. My neck had twisted painfully with the force of the slap, as it made my head turn awkwardly. I cupped my burning ear, trying to dispel the dull ringing sound.

"No, no Andrew please!" I begged him.

He was advancing on me again and so I yelled: "STOP!" I don't know where I found my voice but I did. LEAVE ME ALONE!

JUST GET OUT!" I yelled my voice shaking, not just my voice but my whole body now.

Andrew began raining down hard painful blows upon me one after the other. I don't know how many times, I couldn't count. I remember my hands around my head trying to protect it. I felt a sharp pain in my back. I don't know if it was a punch or a kick. I could taste blood in my mouth; I think it was from biting my lip or tongue I couldn't tell which. He hit me again in my back, this time it caught my breath, winding me. Then he moved on kicking my legs over, and over, and over again. I was crying until he winded me, and then I remember making the horrible deep moaning sound as I tried to breathe, and I began to panic that I was going to die, right there on the floor, with our children in the next room.

I could hear them crying. Andrew did too, and so he shut the living room door. I wanted to go to them, to make them feel better, but I couldn't move. Andrew would not let up his vicious assault on my body.

Caleb was trying to open the living room door

"GO! Back" he yelled at Caleb.

"Please don't yell at him, Andrew. Please" I cried out, and he released me. But it wasn't over. He came striding back, grabbed me by my hair and yanked me up to my knees. In his hand was the heavy stainless steel pan from the draining board. He held it by the handle and brought it up high.

Caleb opened the door, and I saw him at the kitchen doorway looking from me to Andrew, concerned and trying not to cry.

This is it, is all I remember thinking. I am going to die. My body was limp, there was no fight in me whatsoever. I was going to die in front of my son.

"IM GOING TO SPLATTER YOUR BRAINS OUT ALL OVER THIS FLOOR!" He roared.

I am going to die my mind repeated over, and over. I was thinking that I would never be able to hold my children or tell them how much I loved them ever again.

"P please Andrew, if you are going to do it, then please I beg you, not in front of the children. I, ll love t them."

Andrew's eyes followed my own, and he dropped me and dropped the heavy pan.

"I'm sorry." he breathlessly muttered after a minute or so.

I began crawling painfully backward on my hands, and then I tried to get up, by bracing my hands flat against the wall. I managed to drag myself up, but I couldn't fully stand. I was hunched, feeling almost completely broken, but the whole time I could or would not take my eyes off of him.

"I will see to the kid's, go and sort yourself out." He said dejectedly and sighed.

I could hear him in the living room comforting the children, telling them it was all okay. He told Caleb that mummy, and daddy was having a fight, but not to cry, and everything would be alright. I knew he would be cuddling Caleb, and I knew he would be trying to cradle Holly also, who I think was upset because she was waiting for her bottle, and everyone had left her.

Andrew spent the rest of the day trying to be nice to me, and wiping away the fat salty tears that would not cease rolling down my cheeks, and into my mouth. Andrew tried asking me to smile for the children, and told me not let them see me upset; saying that it wasn't good for them, and by saying that it was mother's day, and I should be happy around them.

I did force a smile, not because he told me to, but for my beautiful children, especially for Caleb who had by now forgotten that he was upset, and was happily playing with his toys, or curling up on my lap for a cuddle.

Andrew went to his parent's house a little later on, but not without first taking my purse, and warning me not to leave the flat.

I complied.

Chapter Fifty-Seven

A new friend

By the time Caleb was three Andrew began taking him to work with his father, and brothers once or twice a week for a few hours. Caleb loved sitting in the work van and taking his toy builder set along with him. Andrew would take him along to price jobs, or whilst he was working inside houses. Andrews's father was doing less work now, as he had handed over the physical side of the family business to Andrew and so he would entertain Caleb a lot of the time when they went to look at houses to work on.

I would often take both of the children swimming, to the park, or for birthday parties. We would often visit the duck pond, and feed the ducks, and swans.

∞∞∞

The first September of Caleb's fourth birthday he started pre-school. Preschool was designed to get the children ready, and into a routine for when it was time to begin the first year of school the following year.

I cried that first day, along with several other mums. It was difficult watching your child in school uniform, holding a packed lunch and having to leave you for the whole day, with teachers that you didn't really know. I heard a few mothers commenting on how big their kid's looked, or how they were glad to be rid of them for some peace. I didn't think Caleb looked any older than the day before, and I certainly wasn't looking for peace. I was going to miss him, and his company. I didn't think any less of the parents for their views, everyone's situation is different. They probably had busy lives, and lots of friends to socialize with. I didn't, all I had were my children. They were my smiles, my laughter, my affection and my social life.

I did eventually strike up a friendship with Janice, one of the mum's at the school. Janice's daughter was in the same class as Caleb. Janice and I hit it off more or less instantly. She was slender, with long blonde hair, and big blue eyes. She was funny, straight to the point, no messing and she had great intuition.

Janice knew pretty straight off the bat that I was unhappy, but it took several weeks of her cajoling before I told her a little bit about Andrew, and what was happening.

"My God! You've got to leave the bastard!" she exclaimed in shock.

"I can't Janice it's not that easy. He is the father of my children, they love him, well Caleb does at any rate. Holly, he doesn't bother too much with right now. Besides, I've tried in the past, and he found me and bought me back every single time." I said dejectedly.

"What about your parents?" she asked hopefully, blond eyebrows raised.

"Andrew had me cut my mother off, and his mother thought it was for the best too. She is an alcoholic you see. She works, and she's kind, but he doesn't want myself or the kid's around all that. To be honest Janice I know it's so I can't run back to her. As for my dad, he lives in Spain right now, and he can't really help me."

Janice never pressed me any harder with questions or advice, but she was a wonderful friend, who eventually became my best friend. I would often go round to Janice's with my two, and they would go off an play with her three, whilst we had coffee and discussed our dreams. Janice was married to Keith a quiet, but fairly nice guy, who went fishing... a lot. Janice and Keith argued quite a bit, mostly it was annoyed banter back and forth and they always laughed at each other and quickly made it up.

I had also made friends with two other mum's, Cathy who had a little girl Maddy, and Susan, who had a little boy called Joshua. I would often take Caleb to each of their houses for play dates with his friends. I would drink coffee with each of the mum's, but I never once told them what I had told Janice.

Janice a few months later approached me one morning, after dropping our little ones off.

"I need to speak to you." She said her face full of concern.

"Okay, well let's go get coffee..."

"No, not at yours today, let's make it mine okay?"

And so I got in her car and placed Holly in her younger daughter's car seat, and we set off. Janice was silent all the way there, and by the time we pulled up Holly had started to nod off.

"Here give her to me. I will pop her on the sofa, with a blanket, you go in and pop the kettle on.

As we approached her front door I notice cardboard had been taped over her letterbox.

"Janice, why on earth have you taped up your letterbox with cardboard?"

"Oh, Jesus. That!" she sighed heavily. "The bloody postman put his hand in the letterbox and the dog ripped the guy's finger off. I heard a load of screaming this morning, and as I grabbed Bthe dog I noticed this bloody finger on the floor by the door."

"Oh no!" I exclaimed gasping in horror. "Wait your joking right?"

"No, I'm not joking! Keith had to take him to the hospital to get in sewn back on. God knows what's going to happen, but I have to get one of those basket thingy's that catch the mail, on the inside, as well as a flaming sticker outside, to warn about the dog. Also, Keith has had to put him in the dog kennel out back for now."

"Janice that's terrible! Was he mad?"

"I don't know he was too busy screaming his bollocks off!"

I slapped my hand over my mouth, my eyes wide, and we both laughed. Not so much at the situation, because that was quite serious. It was more the way she said he was screaming his balls off.

"But listen let's get little miss in, and settled because we have to talk." She said firmly.

Once Holly was settled on the sofa, fast asleep, and we had our cuppas, we sat at the kitchen table did Janice speak to me.

I'm so sorry to have to tell you this Evie, but I heard a couple of mums talking yesterday on the way out of the school, just after you left. It was Maddy's mum."

"Maddy's mum?" I asked curiously.

"Yes, I heard her talking, she was telling Joshua's mum that she had slept with Andrew and that she didn't know how to stop you from bringing Caleb round to play with Maddy. It was awkward were her words."

I scanned my mind trying to figure out how he could have slept with her, a married woman, with both of our kid's around. It hit me then. Andrew had gone to pick Caleb up from hers a couple of times after I had dropped him off to play for an hour or two. It was a mutual thing, sometimes I would watch Maddy, whilst her mum did some shopping in the supermarket in the center below the flat.

"It must have been when I had Maddy a couple of days ago," I said in shock. My stomach felt like it had dropped.

It would make sense for her to tell Joshua's mum because they were best friends. Even though she was married, she had told me that she and her husband were seeking a divorce. I thought.

"That skanky little witch!" I hissed angrily.

What could I do I thought? This wasn't the first time. I remembered the note that someone with the initial M had left on his car windshield.

"I just thought you should know. If you want I can have a not so friendly word with her?"

"No, no Janice that won't be necessary, but thanks. I will handle it."

Chapter Fifty-Eight

More Secrets

I later found out that Andrew had been sleeping with other women. I did confront Cathy, Maddy's mother, and she spitefully told me that he had also slept with one of the other mum's that he met, who worked part-time in a pub across the road from the flat.

I specifically remembered that one evening after he got home from the pub, two buttons were missing from his polo shirt, his jeans were ripped, and he had a large red mark on his cheekbone. When I asked him what had happened he had told me that one of the guys in the bar thought that he was trying it on with his missus in the toilet, and they had had a fight. I knew then there was some truth.

I told Cathy to stay away from my family in the future, and to never speak to me again. I eventually figured out who the woman in the pub was. She had a son in the year above Caleb at school, and her son was on the same kid's football team as Caleb too. Andrew would often take him to his game once a week on the playing field, next to the community center, across from the flat.

His philandering ways did not end there, however. A month or so later the house phone rang, and I answered. There was a little bit of static on the other end of the line, and I could hear muffled sounds. I said Hello a few times, asking who was there. I was about to hang up the phone when I heard a click, and Andrews' voice talking to someone, but it sounded like a recording. I listened as he was telling the unknown woman all the things that he wanted to do to her body, and what he wanted her to do to his. I shouted over the phone, asking who it was that was calling me. I got no answer instead the phone clicked on the other end and I got a flat dial tone. Whoever it was, had hung up.

I decided at this point to call Andrew's mother to find out if she knew what Andrew was up to, but she didn't. Instead, she called Andrew on his mobile and told him to come home and speak to me.

Andrew denied everything of course, and he tried to tell me there were hoax calls going about, where people's voices were being recorded and changed to say other things to get the person speaking into trouble.

I was too scared to push him too far, and I knew if I got mad, then he would only do something to me, and turn it back around on me, and so I let it go.

Chapter Fifty-Nine

House Of Ill Repute

A couple of months or so after that I had been visiting with Andrew's mum, and I had decided to get a few things in town before getting the bus home. As I was walking with Holly in her pram I heard someone call out my name. I turned around and I saw Damon, Andrew's best friend Simon's brother. I had only had a few conversations with Simon over the years, and I had only ever seen his brother one time before today. I had never actually spoken to him before now.

He asked me how I was, and we shared some small talk. It seemed odd that he wanted to chat. I didn't know him at all, but I was polite.

He told me that Andrew had been out quite a bit with Simon, and his family was getting concerned about their trips to Brighton. I apologized, as I had no idea where it was they were going to, and I would mention it to Andrew. Damon asked me not to mention anything, and he would try and catch up with Simon. Damon explained that Simon was quite fragile, because of his brain tumor, and that they didn't like him going off so far, especially Brighton without letting his parents know exactly where he was. Even though Simon was an older man, he still needed to be looked out for as his memory was not very good, he was forgetful, and complacent a lot of the time.

I said goodbye to Damon, feeling a little unnerved, and I told Damon that I hoped everything was okay, and I left, getting on my bus.

I kept my promise, and I never said anything to Andrew about seeing Simon's brother earlier on that day. I was busy with the children and it just kind of slipped to the back of my mind.

$$\infty\infty\infty$$

It wasn't until the next day that I got another phone call. I was surprised when Damon told me that it was him, and he was sorry to bother me. I was about to tell him that Andrew was at work when he said it was me that he wished to speak to.

He told me that I was a very nice girl and that he thought it only right that I know what was going on. I felt a little confused and worried as to what he was going to tell me, but I waited, silently.

He asked me if I was still on the phone, to which I responded that I was, and then he told me...

He was ashamed to admit on his brother's behalf that for a couple of years they had been taking Simon once a month to a prostitute in Brighton, as Simon didn't have a girlfriend, and was possibly never going to marry. But the problem was, that Andrew had taken over giving him lifts to the house, where Simon would see one of the girls that worked there. He told me he was sorry, and it wasn't his place to tell me, but like he said I was a nice girl, who didn't deserve what Andrew was doing. He had heard the way Andrew had spoken about me several times to Simon- thing's like he was "only with me for the kid's and that I looked after him almost as good as his mother."

My hand was shaking, holding the telephone. There was too

much talking, he was saying too much, so fast, and I couldn't keep up. I asked him exactly what he was trying to tell me, and after a few seconds of silence, he told me...

Andrew had also been sleeping with prostitutes.

Damon said that I was better off without Andrew and that I should take the kid's and leave him, saying I could do so much better.

Something inside of me just completely snapped, and I ended up yelling at Damon for trying to cause trouble in my marriage. I guess I was more embarrassed than anything, and I tried to play down my emotion by making myself sound angry. I told him to never call me again and to mind his own business.

Chapter Sixty

Nanny, I miss you

I still called my nan once or twice a week. Andrew and I had also gone to visit her on a few occasions over the years. I knew that she didn't like Andrew. She was too much of a lady to say so, but I knew Andrew could tell that she didn't like him. I had never openly spoken to Nan about what Andrew had been doing, and saying to me over the years. I didn't because I knew how very sad it would make her.

When she discovered that I had been sexually abused by Melvin all those years ago, she was very heartbroken. I didn't know until a few years ago that she had approached a social worker when I was in foster care, asking if she could have me stay with her, and keep me. My mother apparently refused the offer, and well you already know what happened to me.

I had to speak to her though. I needed to hear her comforting and familiar voice. I tried to tell her everything, but I was crying too much to be properly understood. My Nan did eventually get the gist of what I was trying to say, and she begged me to leave him and to go and stay with her. But I just couldn't do it. Nan was in her seventies. The last thing she would need was two children running about, and me with no money and no career. I knew she wouldn't really bother about the children, because she loved them, but it wasn't only that. I knew Andrew would come looking for me, and I would not put her through his constant calling, or sitting outside her house in his car, watching and waiting to get me on my own. I didn't feel that she could cope with any of that at all.

Nan asked me if I could go to my mother, but my answer was just the same. He would constantly hound her to, and make her uncomfortable, scared even because Andrew never hid his darker side from her. He threatened me once that if I were to ever try to get in touch with her then he would do something terrible to her, or to me. It wasn't worth the risk.

∞∞∞

So here I was, sat on a chair in the back garden, feeling trapped and unable to turn to anyone for help, and all I could do was cry about it. Even if I did chose to leave him, could I really take his children away from him? Despite how badly he treated me, he did love them very much.

No was the ultimate answer... I couldn't, and I would not do it. I had put myself in this situation, and if I wasn't going to leave it then I had to make peace with what I had chosen, or be dammed for the rest of my life.

If I had of been brave enough to confront him, how would it have made me look? because I knew that I couldn't do anything to stop it, and I wouldn't do anything about it because I was much too afraid of the consequences. Pathetic that's how I would look. I felt like a sad and pathetic woman who was going to say and do nothing, absolutely nothing! That's what.

I went through periods of coming to reasonable options, with regards to leaving or staying with Andrew, and then immediately afterward telling myself how stupid and worthless I was again.

Andrew hadn't beaten me for a while and now I knew why, it was because he was finding happiness elsewhere, and he was hardly ever home in my company. It was then that I had another thought…

If he was going to other women, and he was hardly home then surely that was better for me, and the children?

I spent so much time thinking, coming to conclusions, and then re-questioning the conclusions that I just made myself even more confused, hurt, and angry. I wore myself out with thinking, crying and worrying. Thank God for Janice though because she was always there, and I knew deep down that if ever I needed her help that she would be there, Keith too.

Janice had told Keith about Andrew, and Keith hated him too. He asked me once if I wanted him to put Andrew in his place, by threatening him or something. I said no, but at times like this I wish I had, but I knew if it came right down to it I would back out and ask Keith to forget about it. I think it was very hard for them sometimes, watching me almost coming apart at the seams, and having to listen to what Andrew was doing to me. I had decided to cease talking about Andrew altogether after a while, it wasn't doing any good. I wanted to enjoy my freedom with them, and not sit in front of them crying about all the things that I couldn't or wouldn't change.

The day after I had spoken to my nan, she passed away in her sleep in the hospital, and I was devastated. Nan was well thought of by everyone who knew her, and she was well loved. and Everyone was going to miss her, especially me.

I went to see her a couple of hours before she passed away, and she was trying so hard to tell me something, but I couldn't understand what she was trying to say through the noise of her oxygen mask, and her tiredness.

I was devastated.

Chapter Sixty One

Getting in deeper

A few months later I noticed a change in Andrew. He was home a lot more. He was spending more time playing with the children, and he was beginning to spend more time with me. If I was sitting in the living room, he would sit down next to me. If I was in the kitchen, he would stand to talk to me. Most of our conversations revolved around work, his parents or our children, and then a little later he would talk about our relationship. He wanted for us to go out more together as a couple, or as a family.

I was, of course, agreeable, or complaint I really didn't know which one, to be honest.

I was tidying away the children's toys one afternoon when Andrew sat down in one of the armchairs, with a long sigh.

"I have been thinking... do you want to get married?" I could literally feel the hair rising on my head and arms. No, I didn't really want to get married, and I hadn't ever thought about it either. Not for a very long time. But that's not how I responded. Instead, I answered with what I thought he wanted me to answer and that was...

"Yes, okay."

I got a phone call from his mother the next day, as she wanted to discuss the wedding arrangements. Andrew had told her that he wanted to get married in a registry office, and we were to keep it small. Andrew had whilst at worked booked a date in July.

His mother had organized the reception to be held in a pub where she was working as a cleaner. Andrews sister in law who was heavily into painting or decorating glassware at the time had offered to make a few centerpieces for the tables. Andrew's mother organized a cake with a friend of hers. It was fruit, with hard icing. I didn't mind the fruit, but I really couldn't stand the icing, but I agreed anyway, after all, it was only a cake!

The only items I was free to choose was my wedding dress, which had to be no more than one hundred pounds, and I was to choose an outfit for Caleb and a dress for Holly too.

I took Janice off with me for a trip into Brighton to have a look at some wedding dress shops. I was shocked that they were all so expensive; some of them were worth thousands of pounds, and I think the cheapest one we saw that day was about six hundred pounds.

"You'll maybe have to look in the Friday-Ad to see if you can get a wedding dress second hand," Janice said rather pensively, on the way home.

As it happened I did find a dress. I was on my way to return some books a the library, and next door was a small charity shop. In the front window was a white satin dress, with an off the shoulder look, and a sweetheart neckline. It wasn't something I would have actually picked, but beggars couldn't be choosers and so I went in to try it on. It turned out to be a little bit baggy on the waistline, and the chest was a little tight, but not bad. I returned the books as I was meant to, and returned home with a wedding dress for twenty pounds. I even found a small tiara that was three pounds and a pair of off white sandals.

I imagined Andrew being very pleased when I was to tell him

how much money I had saved, but he didn't come home for dinner.

I ate with the children, gave them their baths and read them each a story for bed. There was still no Andrew. I decided to call his mother to see if she knew where he was, but she didn't. Apparently, he dropped his dad and brother off after work and told them he would see them the next day, and that was it.

"He will turn up; he probably went to the pub or to meet Simon." She said. "Have you tried his mobile?"

"No. I thought I would see if he was still at yours." I responded a little flatly. "But I will let you know if he's still not back later on." And with that we each hung up.

As soon as she mentioned Simon and the pub, I knew she was probably right. Andrew and Simon used to go into the town every Friday after work for drinks. Well, it was good of him to let me know I thought. It didn't take him long to revert back to his ways. I scraped off his now dried up dinner and threw it in the bin. I did some tidying up and watched TV on the sofa until I fell asleep. It was just after 2 am when I awoke to the sound of Andrew closing the front door. I sat up bleary-eyed, waiting for him to see me on the sofa, and he did.

"Where have you been?" I asked him. "I called your mother, and she didn't know where you were either." I could tell he was drunk by his stagger.

"I was out with Simon. Why you got a problem with that?" he said with a drunken sneer.

"I had to throw your dinner in the bin. It went dry." I said with a little more brevity than I actually felt.

"I can do what I bloody well want. I don't need your permission." He said stabbing a finger out towards me. He then turned around, taking himself off to bed.

The next day I went round to see Janice, and as usual, the kid's went off to play with her three. I busied myself helping her to peel the vegetables for their Sunday dinner.

"What's happened?" she asked me wistfully.

"Andrew has started going out again with Simon, without telling me anything. I had to throw his dinner away last night, and when I told him I really thought he was going to go for me." I replied, gently biting my lip.

"Evie." She sighed. "Why are you going to marry him?"

"It's complicated... It would be nice to have the same surname as my children. Do you know how many people have asked me if the children are mine? But, it's not just that. Maybe this is all I have left. What else can I do?"

"Evie I want you to remember I said this okay? You have two beautiful kids, and what they need is a happy mother. You are going to spend the rest of your life with a man who doesn't love you, and only mildly cares for you, because you are giving him children, and taking care of him. You could be spoiling your chance of any future happiness, just so you can make him happy."

"Janice. I know what you are saying, but I can't leave. I can't leave because he is their father. What will it do to them?"

"Evie, you can't always look out for other people. You need to look out for yourself too. One day your kid's will be grown up. They will move out, and then where will you be? And that's if he doesn't finish you off!" she said more passionately.

I hung my head and then looked out of her kitchen window. I was trying so hard not to cry. I felt Janice's hand on my shoulder, and I couldn't hold back my tears, my anger, my hurt, and my frustration.

∞∞∞

I was sitting in front of my Doctor, calmly clasping my hands.

"Evie are you sure that this is what you want? you are asking me for a reversable sterilisation?"

"Yes that is what I am asking for." I said swallowing deeply.

"Evie you are only twenty one?" the Doctor looked at me as if I was crazy or something.

I knew what I was doing. I had decided that no matter what, I would not give birth to anymore of Andrew's children, especially not after he had kicked me when I was pregnant with Holly. I was so afraid that I had lost her.

A few months later I had Filche clips placed on my fallopian tubes. I told Andrew that there was a problem with them and that I had to have the clips, as it was dangerous if I got pregnant again.

Andrew didn't seem bothered at all, and I knew with a firmness that I had made the right decision.

Chapter Sixty Two

Meltdown

I got a frantic phone call a few days later, it was Andrew's mother. Andrew had had an accident. He had been lifting some heavy paving slabs, and somehow he had tripped and one of his fingers was almost completely severed off. His father had taken him straight to the hospital, and he was having it sewn back on. I was told not to panic, stay with the children, and just to look after him when he got home.

After hanging up I know this must sound completely awful, but I laughed. The children were at first just staring at me, and because I was laughing, they too began laughing, and they made me laugh harder. I laughed so hard that tears were pouring down my face. I tried to stop, but I couldn't. I knew it was shameful of me, and I felt terrible after I had calmed myself down. I remember thinking who does that?! Oh my God, I'm having a bloody meltdown, for sure!

By the time Andrew came home, I was fully composed. I ooh'd, ahh'd and spoke to him soothingly. I offered to sleep on the sofa so that I didn't bump his overly large bandaged thumb by accident in the night. He agreed.

Every time I heard him wince (which was a lot) or hold his breath in pain I had to hide my smirks. I remember thinking at the time…. how does it feel to be in pain Andrew? I was also thinking that I was sure that I had felt a lot more pain, through his beating's, than he did in that finger, and I didn't go complaining or rolling about. I still had two children, as well as him, a house to care for, and shopping to do.

∞∞∞∞

I have to say that I have never been in the unlucky position of losing a digit. I do not doubt that it is very dangerous and even painful. At the time they were my most honest, inner thoughts, towards a man who was over the years very cruel towards me. I don't think it really is laughable for that to happen to a person. I don't know why I laughed so hysterically. It was totally out of character even for me. The only way I can describe what I was experiencing was some form of meltdown.

Despite my secret thoughts, I did take care of him, and a few weeks later we married in Lewes registry office. It was a small gathering, not even the slightest bit intimate, and there was no honeymoon.

Chapter Sixty-Three

A little bit of freedom

L ife had gone on in much the same fashion over the next year. Andrew was out every weekend going to nightclubs with his mates. I didn't know if he was still visiting the prostitutes in Brighton. Every Sunday we would have dinner with his parents. Caleb was now in his first year at school, and Holly was going to nursery school. I had got myself a job as the sole cleaner in the small Doctor's surgery a two-minute walk from the flat.

One afternoon I went inside the shopping center supermarket, as Holly was in need of a new pair of shoes, and so I went to an independent shoe shop within the supermarket. I began chatting with the manager, and her work friend. We all ended up chatting for a good hour. Before I left with my purchase, the manager offered me a new full-time job, and I felt quite excited.

The manager let me start my shifts through the week after I had taken Caleb to school and dropped Holly off at nursery school. I would work for three hours, and then go and pick Holly up after lunchtime, and then I would go back again at 5 pm, when Andrew was home, and work until the shop closed at 8 pm.

Andrew didn't seem to happy that he would have to be home to look after the kids, but he didn't complain. I thought maybe it was my own independence that he didn't like. I expected him to tell me to forget it, but I think he was at the point now where he just didn't care what I did, so long as I remained there with him, and the children.

∞∞∞∞

I took up reading at home, instead of the library mainly because I just didn't have the time, but I still loved to get lost in the pages once the children were in bed. Reading seemed to take me to a whole other world. I was reading as if I was the main character, seeing and feeling every emotion that they did. I would be in another time, or another place.

Janice asked me one day what I was reading now, and It was actually a book about spirituality, clairvoyance, psychics and how to become one.

Janice told me that was strange because she had lots of dreams about events that had actually occurred within her own life. I told her that I had been trying to meditate, but the only place I could do it was in the bath, as I had no privacy anywhere else.

We began trying to meditate together, buying crystals, placing them on our foreheads over our third eye. I have to say we both saw some strange faces, and wonderful shapes and colors.

Janice found a small spiritualist group. A lady ran it from her house, not too far from the flat, and so we went. Her living room was dim, and there were lit candles everywhere. I could smell the sweet, strong smell of pot puri, which actually turned out to be incense burning. There were six of us, in total including the lady, and everyone was sitting comfortably around her living room, some were sitting on the floor, with their legs crossed. I really didn't know how serious to take it all, but everyone was really kind and soft-spoken. My body just seemed to instantly relax whenever I was there.

After the meditation sessions, Janice would become so hyped about what she had seen and trying to figure out what it all meant. I used to just look at her and think Wow you're so hooked!.

Andrew thought what I was doing was stupid, and he thought that Janice was stupid to for getting me into all that crap, as he called it. But I didn't think it was crap at all.

I could not explain why I was seeing the faces of strangers when I meditated. I could not explain the things that I was beginning to hear in my head but in my own thoughts, it was very strange to me, and I just didn't get it at all. I tried to convince myself that my mind was making it all up, or maybe the people in the group were making me believe I was seeing and hearing things because I wanted to.

Janice decided to buy a Ouija board, to commune with the spirit world. I had heard a lot of dangerous and negative things about using Ouija board's -like letting in negative spirits or even the devil himself. That wasn't all. Apparently, if you didn't open and close the Ouija correctly then the spirits could stay and cause all kinds of destruction in your life, such as messing with your emotions, and things around the home. I was petrified, but Janice had assured me that she knew exactly what she was doing, and so... one evening we decided to give it a go.

We were sat in her darkened kitchen with a couple of candles placed either side of the board. The house was silent. Janice spoke an opening prayer asking our spirit guides to keep us safe and to let no spirit remain afterward.

I could feel my mouth going dry. I was scared even to breathe with my finger opposite hers on the planchette. Within moments I could feel the planchette moving underneath my finger, and I snatched my hand away.

"Evie! Don't take your finger off!" exclaimed Janice.

"That was you, moving it!" I said wide-eyed looking at her face for some sort of give away.

"It bloody well was not! put your finger back and let's see who it is." She said excitedly.

"Okay, but I'm watching you, Janice," I said seriously, but with a squint in her direction.

The planchette moved once again, sometimes fast pointing towards letter, and sometimes a little slower. Janice was trying to keep up with writing what the letters were spelling. It just seemed like gobbly goop.

"That was intense." She said afterward, looking as serious as I was.

In that instant, we both screamed as Keith flicked on the kitchen light. Keith got the fright of his life and then said gruffly...

"What the bloody hell are you two up to now?"

Janice and I looked at each other and burst out in fits of laughter. I think Keith was more annoyed because we made him jump, and his departing words were...

"You are bloody mad you two." And we laughed even harder.

Before I left to go home I popped my head around their living room door. Keith was sitting at his computer on a fishing forum.

"Hey, Keith. Sorry, we made you jump." I grinned

Keith looked around at me and laughed.

" If there are bumps, and spooks in the night, you can blame your wife." I giggled cheerfully.

"If there are, then I'm sending them back." He said grinning with a cheeky wink.

Chapter Sixty Four

Enough

J anice dropped me off. The time was later than I thought. But for the first time in a long time, I felt carefree and happy. It was a different kind of happy. I loved the children and they made me feel loved and happy. I laughed with them a lot, but what I was feeling now was a different kind of happy. It was my first evening out without Andrew or the kid's... ever, and I think I was finding myself...

"What time do you call this?" Andrew spoke darkly, from the living room doorway.

I apologized for it being so late, and I did so with a sort of sympathetic frown, and I tried to smile.

"You're a slag." He spat angrily.

I don't remember everything he said to me that night, but I do remember being slammed into the hallway cupboard; I felt a sharp stinging down the length on my forearm, where I had grazed it on the sharp, round knob, as I slid down it. I felt several hard stinging slaps on my face, and more on, and about my head. I had my eyes closed tightly and I raised my arms to try and protect my head, but it was useless.

I began to hear a low guttural screaming sound, and at the same time, my body began charging forwards. The sound I realized was me. I sounded like some sort of wildling. I had a tight hold of Andrews' forearms and I was pushing him backward, all the way into the living room, where he landed on the sofa. He managed to get back up, and he came at me again. I could see his fingers trying to claw for my face. He managed to grab a hold of me, and once more I felt him slapping and punching about my head, and my arms. I was still trying to push him back, and then I found myself being flung around, and again I pushed into him. He fell, and then I fell on top of him. I got my knees either side of him, and I hit him over, and over, and over again. I don't know how many times or for how long. I was hitting him so fast, not giving him a chance to fight me back. This time he was the one cowering and trying to cover his body.

I remember yelling at him, as I pummeled him over and over... "DON'T YOU EVER FUCKING TOUCH ME!! DON'T YOU EVER TOUCH ME YOU FILTHY DIRTY BASTARD! "

I never thought about the consequences of my actions. I wasn't thinking about anything except my blind rage and keeping him from hurting me. I was running out of breath, and my arms were aching and my hands were burning.

I got up from him, my chest heaving, and my body trembling from pain, exhaustion, adrenaline? I have no idea. Maybe it was a combination of the three.

We glared at each other. I was standing, and he was on the floor. I guess I was waiting, waiting for him to get up, and go for me again. If he did I knew that there was nothing left in me to either defend or protect myself. I took a step backward.

"I'm done, we are finished," I said my voice sounding harsh, and croaky. My throat felt like sandpaper, and my tongue felt bone dry. My breathing was still a little ragged.

Andrew's face was pink, and there were scratch marks from my nails on his cheek.

It did cross my mind that he was just biding his time and waiting to catch me unawares, but I bravely walked past him into the living room, and I sat down heavily in an armchair. Andrew got up and walked into the living room, and he began pacing the floor.

I was still waiting for him to come at me. I was not going to believe that he would let me retaliate on him, and let me get away with it. I knew he was thinking and planning a course of action, and so I spoke to try and distract him.

"Andrew I don't want to live like this anymore. We can't live like this anymore. It's not fair on either of us." I said slowly, and calmly.

"What are you saying?" he asked angrily.

"We don't love each other. You have never really loved me. Don't you want to be with someone that you're in love with? Don't I deserve the same, to be happy? We can't live like this. I have nothing left anymore. It's gone."

I was so so afraid, but I couldn't stop myself from telling him.

I could see his bottom lip starting to tremble, and the same look he had given me many times after going too far, and he tried to make me feel sorry for him.

"Don't you love me then?" he asked like he was about to sob.

There were several seconds of silence before I managed to croak fearfully "No Andrew I don't. I tried to. I wanted so badly to love you. Andrew, I already know you don't love me, and it's not fair to keep me like this. It's not fair for our children. They will want us to be happy to, not living like this. They are going to get older, and see what you are doing to me."

Andrew bowed his head and he began to cry. As I watched him I felt nothing, no sadness, and no shame. I found my brave.

Andrew abruptly got up, and went to our bedroom, and closed the door quietly behind him.

Chapter Sixty-Five

Limbo

Andrew and I barely spoke over the next few days. We had a lilac colored futon at the opposite end of the living room, and I had now made that my bed. I took out all my clothes from the wardrobe, and drawers and I kept them in a cupboard in the hallway, and under the futon bed.

I continued every day getting up, and seeing to the children, and going work. Andrew did the same. Nothing much had changed. I couldn't afford to rent another place, and Andrew I guessed didn't want to go back to his mother's.

I had decided to save as much as I could through my job, and what was left of the shopping money and after Holly's nursery fee's, and try to make a fresh start. I would not go to anyone for help, just in case Andrew decided to do what he had always done, stalked, pestered and followed me until I would give in. This time I would get somewhere of my own, not tell him where, and arrange for him to see the children at his parents or something. I didn't have every single detail figured out, but it was at least something.

I had found a spiritual group online, and I joined in their group chats, mostly in the evenings when Andrew had gone to bed.

When I next saw Janice, she could tell instantly that there was something different about me. I told her what had happened. I told her that Andrew and I had ended up in some sort of bar-room brawl after she had dropped me off after the Ouija session. She looked genuinely shocked, and she said that she couldn't believe that I had in me to stand up to him... neither could I really. It was a dangerous risk.

"So what, you're just going to stay living with him, for how long?" she asked, her eyebrows raised.

"As soon as I can I guess. I've considered getting a credit card so I can come up with a deposit for a new place, but... I don't know. I will probably be unable to afford the re-payment, along with all the other bills as well.

"Get Andrew to stump something up. He will at least have to give you money for the children." Janice said hopefully."

"He won't Janice. The last time I left he said he couldn't afford to give me anything, he said if I tried to claim he would just tell the CSA that he had no work or money. I don't want anything from him anyway, because then I don't need to thank him."

"Wait, they will check his bank though won't they?" she asked angrily

"Yes, but his Dad gets the money in cash or cheques, and he pays his son's in cash, avoiding a bank trail."

"What a knob!" she muttered. "Andrew I mean." She added as an afterthought.

"Yep" I agreed with a sigh.

Chapter Sixty-Six

A message from the other side

Once a week, there was an indoor market, which was set up in a big room, within the shopping center. The room reminded me of a large school assembly hall. Over the years I had been going to an elderly lady who ran a children's stall. I had gotten Holly lots of pretty outfits from her, and each time she grew out of them I gave them back. I never took any money back for them; instead, she used to give me discounts on other clothes. I would always browse the book stalls, being a total book-worm. I would also check out kid's videos, and games. I loved second-hand things. New things were nice, but I used to think why should I pay full price for something? when I could get it cheaper. I used to call it treasure hunting, there was an old saying about someone's rubbish was another's treasure... or something like that.

As I was walking around I noticed a middle-aged lady staring at me from behind her stall, which was full of crystals and things. Normally seeing a stall like that I would have gone straight over, but I didn't want to. The lady made me feel so uncomfortable.

As I was walking out, past her table she said...

"Excuse me dear?" with a wide smile.

I stopped and turned to face her.

"Have you got a moment? I have to tell you something?" she

reached out her arm to me, still smiling.

I felt myself stiffen a little, but I obliged her.

I followed her behind her stall and she pointed me to one of the two chairs behind the table.

"Would you mind? My husband is not here at the moment. I'm very sorry to approach you like this, as I would never normally do this, but I feel that I have to."

"Okay. I will stand though if you don't mind; as I haven't got long I need to get back home." I said kindly, wondering what all this was about. I was now wondering if she wanted some sort of help.

"I am a clairvoyant. It means that I can see spirit, loved ones. Please don't think I'm some sort of crazy old woman." She said looking mildly embarrassed, if not slightly pained.

"It's okay. I said warily." I know what a Clairvoyant is. I am part of a Spiritualist group."

"There is an older lady with me in Spirit, she says she is your Nan."

I sucked a breath in, and I felt my whole body sort of prickling, but then I thought... what if she is trying it on, or trying to sell me a reading?

"Your Nan, she hasn't been in spirit long. There was something wrong with her lungs like it was difficult for her to breathe, and she said something to you before she passed and you were upset because you didn't know what she was trying to say to you?"

"Okay," I said. I was suddenly feeling soo full of emotion. I loved, my Nan, the sadness of her passing was sometimes a little too much to bear, and I missed her so much. I wanted so badly for the clairvoyant to tell me more because she was right, and I was desperate to hear her words through another.

"Your Nan says she saw you crying. You were sitting on the end of a bed with your face in your hands. She says she was with you, holding you." She said almost in a whisper.

Oh my! I was crying, yesterday, just as this lady had said. I was now holding back my tears, by swallowing the sobs, but I couldn't stop the silent tears that blurred my eyes.

"Your Nan says she is working on it, and I am seeing a tallish man in some sort of armor."

Okay, she almost lost me there. Nan was sending me what... a knight? I was in the real world, not a fairytale. Maybe Nan was trying to make a joke though?... yes maybe that was it.

I thanked the lady very much. I bought an oval-shaped crystal, rose quartz, in baby pink.

"That's very apt. Thank you." Was all she said.

I got home, and I fell to pieces. I wished Nan was there right then. I longed for her to hold me like she did when I was little. I missed the smell of her sweet, musky perfume. I missed her smile... I missed her.

That evening, not long after dinner Andrew went to what was now his room. He went straight there on the nights that he wasn't out unless I was in which case he would sit in the living room.

I signed into the new spiritual group which I had joined recently, and I began chatting with some new friends. In particular Louise and Liz, they were the owners of the group. I ended up in a private chat room with them, and we became fast friends. I did open up a little and I told them a little about Andrew, and that I was now separated pending a new place to live, and a divorce.

God knows how I was going to pay for a divorce I remember thinking.

They were both very sympathetic and they, in turn, told me thing's about their lives that they wouldn't have normally just discussed with anyone else, besides their families. Out of both Louise and Liz, it was Liz that I felt the closest to. I think because she had two children like me, and she was also married.

Louise considered herself to be very knowledgeable about all things spiritual, and she wanted to make more of the group. Maybe even a website with forums for like-minded spiritualists to get together.

I thought that it was a wonderful idea. Louise began talking about all of her ideas for the website, such as online workshops. Louise wanted to assign Liz and I roles, to help out.

I thought it was so lovely, and I was very excited about her ideas, as was Liz. Though I really didn't think I could really help out too much at the time, as there was just so much going on in my life. I didn't want to promise to give my time to something, for which I couldn't. Louise was very sweet and was happy to let me come and help out whenever I could though.

Over the next few days, I was emailed all sorts of links from Louise. She had actually gone and got herself a website. She was very excited, and I felt very proud of her.

Over the coming days we each gave the other our phone numbers, and whenever the kids were in bed or playing in the garden at the weekends, we would be talking to each other on the phone. I eventually agreed to hop on a train to meet Liz in person, and Andrews Mother offered to look after the children.

∞∞∞

As soon as I got off the train I was searching for Liz's description, short, with brown/red hair. Whilst she was looking for me. I spotted her and I called out her name apprehensively. We each sort of jogged to the other and gave each other a big hug. Liz was older than me by a few years. She wore this bright smile, which crinkled up to her eyes.

I met her husband Colin, their two boys, and their family dog. We spent the whole day chatting about so many things. We laughed so much, and I stayed to eat dinner with them before setting off on the train back.

I decided to call Louise that night, and before the end of the conversation, I offered my help with the website, posting the odd thing's here or there to do with meditation and crystals. Which made her very happy, as well as excited, but for me, it meant a lot of reading and lots of typing. But that was okay. I was happy, that everyone was happy.

Chapter Sixty-Seven

Spreading my wings

I had a distinct feeling that Andrew had met someone. Of course, it felt awkward; we were still married, and living together. Andrew and I treated each other more like flat-mates, who only saw each other in passing. I wasn't hurt, or upset. I had no right to be; after all, I told him that I no longer loved him. I guess I just felt... sad. The situation we were in didn't seem appropriate anymore.

∞∞∞∞

Janice and I still saw each other every day at the school. We would still meet up at the spiritualist group. I had given up reading books in favor of writing articles for the website. The children were happy, they didn't seem to catch on to the new arrangements between Andrew, and I. Everyone seemed happy, and in a small way so was I.

I got talking to a wonderful lady on the site, her name was Jane. Jane had joined the site with her son Steve. Jane had a love of Angels, and she was interested in aromatherapy. I too had an interest in aromatherapy, and so I asked her lots of questions.

I eventually got chatting with Steve too. Steve actually turned out to be Louise's stepbrother. He seemed like such a nice guy. There were only really a handful of men on the site, and most of them were older. Steve, however, was only a couple of years older than me.

∞∞∞∞

As the months went by our friendship grew, and we spoke to each other every day online, as well as on the phone. We talked about everything and anything, and we discovered that we had so much in common.

Steve had told me that he was heavily into LARP's (live-action role-playing). I had absolutely no idea what any of that meant, and so he explained...

Steve was a part of a LARP group, and they would often go to different locations, mainly somewhere with a field and play out scenes that were set for them, as part of a storyline. Every player had developed different characters, and Steve... he played a knight!

I remembered what the Clairvoyant had told me about my nan working on something, and the clairvoyant said that she saw a knight, and I was a little bit stunned!

No, no way I remember thinking this is just too much of a coincidence or was it?

I dd like Steve, but I wasn't looking for any sort of a fling, romance or even love, but... I really quite liked him.

∞∞∞∞

You would maybe think that by this point in my life that I would have nothing more to do with men, or that I would be too scared and untrusting, and well... I did think and feel that initially the first few months of talking to him, but I had absolutely no control over my growing feelings for Steve. None whatsoever.

I did try, by avoiding going online at the same time that I knew he would be on, and by not answering many of his messages. It seemed that the only way that I could avoid Steve and my feelings was to leave the spiritualist group altogether. I did, I tried, but... I missed him because he was above all else my very good friend, and I continued to talk with him.

I told Janice about Steve, and she would often tease me about being in love, and I would tell her to get out, it wasn't like that! And she would carry on teasing me. Eventually, I would just tell her to shut up, and we would laugh about it, like a couple of silly school kids.

"We are going on a trip! Janice announced out of the blue."

"Oh, we are? Okay, where?" I asked perplexed.

If I haven't mentioned it before now I will. Janice had a smile full of big teeth, and whenever she smiled, it would make me smile because she looked goofy. Her teeth were her trademark. I could always pick her out of a smiling crowd.

"We are going to Dudley castle with a ghost tours company. We, my friend... are going ghost hunting!" and there it was! Her, toothy, goofy grin.

Okay, I really liked the sound of it, there was just one small snag. I would have to leave the children with Andrew for the night, and even though he had been okay around me lately, I just didn't know if he would be agreeable.

Janice was okay with me inviting Liz and Louise. I thought

it would be great for them to all meet. Sadly the two girls couldn't make it, but Andrew did agree to mind the children.

Janice and I went shopping with all the kid's, and we managed to get a couple of cheap rucksacks, and some sturdy shoes, as well as a couple of torches and spare batteries.

Chapter Sixty-Eight

Spooks in the night

J anice and I set off super early the following weekend. It was around a three to four-hour journey, by train, and by bus.

The evening was, to begin with, a nighttime walk about the castle as well as the grounds. Then we were going to be taught how to use EVP (electrical voice phenomenon) there was also to be a medium artist who could draw whoever was around you in spirit at that time. Then there was to be supper, an afterward a séance. The rest of the evening into the morning hours was to be a vigil.

We turned up about four hours too early. We ended up going to the local cemetery, to see if we could pick up on any spirits ourselves. I was very tired though, and so I lay down on a patch of grass and used my backpack for a pillow. Janice was flabbergasted.

"What are you doing, going to sleep in a bloody cemetery?" She asked

" I was awake nearly all night with excitement, and now I'm so tired. I can barely keep my eyes open. Besides I'm not lying on top of a grave am I? I can't go to sleep sitting on a bench outside the castle, they might mistake me for a homeless person, and start throwing me spare change." I smiled innocently.

"You are mad. Well, you sleep, and I'll keep watch." She

laughed, as she sat down next to me.

"Janice?"

"Yes?" she replied slowly

"Why do you have to keep watch?" I asked with a smirk.

"Have you ever heard of the term waking the dead?" she asked, her eyebrows rose.

"Yes, but... I somehow doubt that we are going to make enough noise to awaken them" I said, closing my heavy-lidded eyes, and I fell asleep.

I awoke sometime later to Janice frantically shaking me.

"Did you sleep?" I asked bleary-eyed

"Did I shite, get your arse up, it starts in half an hour." She said smiling.

"So you sat, and watched over me just like my guardian angel did you, Janice?" I smirked, batting my lashes. "Thanks, Mum".

"Piss off! And yes! She laughed. "I am not sleeping in no cemetery." And off she stalked through the grass, back towards the gate with me following behind... smirking.

"I do love you, Janice," I whispered.

"Shut up. I love you too." She looked back at me and grinned.

As we walked the tour with about twenty other people I thought about Steve. He would have loved to be here, experiencing all of this. We had joked the day before about me being scared to sleep in a haunted castle (yes even though I slept in a cemetery... but it was daylight.) Steve had jokingly said how he would be my knight in shining armor, by standing guard beside me all night. More like a knight in tin foil. I joked, and we laughed about it.

"You're grinning again!" Janice commented, and I stuck out my tongue.

"I miss talking to Steve. Did I show you his profile picture?"

"Like twenty times." She teased.

"Is it wrong?" I asked quietly, but with a note of sadness.

"Is what wrong? You, liking Steve? No of course not. You have every right to be happy, you deserve to be happy."

"I'm still married, and we still live under the same roof."

"He knows your situation though... right??"

"Yes, well he knows that Andrew and I are separated and that we sleep in different rooms. I've said that I work to pay my half of everything."

"So he really, seriously likes you?"

"Yes, but I don't know Janice. He lives on his own, three hundred miles away. I just don't know how it would work. I can't exactly afford to visit him every weekend, and I can't expect him to drive to see us either. But He has asked me to go and see him for a visit if I wanted to." I couldn't keep myself from smiling a little in embarrassment.

"Well go then!." Janice smiled encouragingly at me.

" I can't. I mean what about the children and Andrew? Andrew would never agree. He would be furious."

"He has no right to be! Anyway, he's moved on, hasn't he? So it's okay for him to sleep around the entire time you have been together, not to mention other women you know, but now you have separated it's not okay for you to move on with another man?" asked Janice, almost hissing in anger.

I loved Janice; she was more like a sister than a best friend. I loved her honesty, and her passion... we were very much alike... two peas in a pod.

"Look if you are worried about Andrew, then just don't tell him. I have an idea... he didn't have a problem with you and I coming to Dudley right?"

"well... no," I answered cautiously.

"Okay, well then just tell him that we are going on a ghost hunting weekend where Steve lives!"

"Janice" I gasped "I can't do that." The idea was crazy because for one what if he saw Janice somewhere when she was supposed to be with me halfway up the country!

"What if he sees you, or Keith. What if he sees Keith and starts talking to him about where we are?"

"I will explain it to Keith. Don't worry he won't give you away, and as for me, I will just stay home. I won't go anywhere unless it's an emergency, and I will be very careful."

I felt stunned by the whole idea. It was so clandestine... but I liked it. I could feel warmth threading its way right into my cheeks, and I grinned.

"I like it. You know it may actually work. But oh my God Janice I'm so nervous. What if he sees me, then changes his mind. I mean I have kids! I've got bloody stretch marks!"

Janice stopped and held both hands out as if she was stopping traffic. It was comical to see.

"You are bloody gorgeous! And who gives a damn about your love streaks! I don't think it's those he would be interested in anyway." She said gently spanking me on the rear.

I gasped "Janice you bugger." And we both laughed, getting out of breath walking up a large grassy knoll.

"I am worried though Janice. What if this turns into something more serious? I don't think Andrew is going to accept it quietly. He may try and cause trouble."

"Well he can try, and hopefully he will fail. Evie... what has Steve said about your kids?"

"Oh, he's fine about me having the children. He actually has a few nieces and nephews, and he has a nice family too by the sounds of it. I already know his mother Jane, and his step-sister Louise. I'm nervous about meeting the rest of his family. I mean what they will think of me being still you know... married?"

"You are sep-a-rated." She exaggerated.

I didn't respond, and we spent the rest of the night enjoying the castle and trying to imagine what it would be like in days old, living there. Janice envisioned herself as being a rich mistress, and she envisioned me as a quiet servant, cleaning out the fireplaces.

When it was time to leave the next morning, we thanked our hosts, said goodbye to the people on the tour that we had chatted with, and headed for the bus stop.

I was so tired on the bus ride to the train station, that I was having a hard time trying to stay awake. I remembered that I kept falling asleep, and every time my head dropped down, I woke up. I did this several times, before finally dozing off.

I awoke with a start, as the bus braked quite hard and I banged my head on the STOP button, setting off the bell to stop the bus.

"Ouch!" I exclaimed

"You silly bugger," Janice said, sniggering, and the bus pulled in to stop. "Not this one love, sorry! She called out to the driver. "My friend accidentally pressed the bell."

I sat rubbing my head, whilst smirking at Janice.

"I'll be glad to get back on my futon tonight. I will never complain about it being lumpy, after lying on that concrete floor."

Chapter Sixty Nine

Cold Feet

I found myself living just for the sound of Steve's voice, every single day. I would think of him all the time. He was my first thought in the morning and my last thought at night before I fell asleep. He sent me a song "Love walked in" by Thunder. I listened to it on repeat Several times a day. I wished so often that I could see him physically. All I had was his picture and the sound of his voice.

∞∞∞

On Monday after the Dudley trip, Steve called me whilst on his lunch break at work. He was so sincerely concerned about me, and the children having to live under the same roof as Andrew, that he made me an offer...

"Look if you ever need somewhere to stay, even if you change your mind and don't want to be with me, you can always stay with me. I have three spare rooms, the children can have one each, and if you want, a room of your own."

He was just so beautiful to me at that moment, so selfless, so caring. I know that we hadn't met each other officially, but his words made me fall in love with him even more. I felt this huge painful lump in my throat, and I could not immediately respond to him. I tried to swallow away the burning lump, and I managed to say Thank you. I couldn't stay talking on the phone anymore; I was too full of emotion. He promised to call me on my shift at work later that afternoon, and we hung up.

I knew I was completely in love, however, there was still a niggling in the back of my mind, that what if all this, with Steve, was just too good to be true. I tried to reason with myself that, his mum Jane couldn't say enough about how caring and kind he was, and then there was also his stepsister Louise, who also sang his praises. It seemed that everyone he spoke to seemed to have nothing but good and positive thing's to say about him. In the end, I came to the conclusion that he loved his family, and they all loved him, and no one had a bad thing to say about him at all.

However, I began to feel afraid, and insecure. I thought maybe it would be better if I was living on my own with the children, and then maybe pursue a relationship with him. I also worried that maybe it would all be too much for Steve, the traveling, having the children around. I had to think of my children, they were my priority, they had to come first. Then I thought of Andrew, maybe he was just being okay because he still had the children here. I knew deep down that if I was to move on with them and begin a relationship with someone new, that he was going to be furious, and possibly dangerous. I didn't think that I wanted to put Steve through that. He didn't deserve it, and so... I had made the awful heartbreaking decision, to let Steve go.

I told him a lie. I told him that I was going to give my marriage a go, for the children, and I was putting them first. I didn't want to tell him that I couldn't do anything because I was too afraid, and I knew he would probably be able to talk me around. He was very honorable when I told him I was giving my marriage a try for the children, and he was so terribly upset, but he said I had to do what was best for me and the children. He said that the children were important and as long as we were all happy, then that's all that mattered.

Chapter Seventy

Lost

Weeks went by. I felt like I was drifting along in a sea of perpetual misery. The only moments that I took joy in, were those spent with my children. I still went onto the site and delivered written workshops on various spiritual topics. I would be able to see if Steve was on-line or not, and when he was I would cry. All I wanted was hear the sound of his comforting voice. I missed him so much, and I wondered if he was missing me too.

I bought Caleb a small bike, and I thought it was a good time to start teaching him how to ride it. After several attempted efforts, he got the hang of it, and he was soon off whizzing around the car park, below the flats. I took to obsessively cleaning and tidying in a bid to keep myself busy. I stopped playing the song that Steve sent me... "Love walked in" by thunder" and I even asked my boss for more shifts. I was now going back to work after Holly had finished nursery, and I was allowed to bring her with me. I set her up in the big office out the back where they kept all the shoes. Holly loved it, as she got to play in all the empty boxes, and she enjoyed scribbling in her coloring in books. Whenever a customer would come in I would go out to quickly serve them, and go back into the office to organize all the shoes and do the stock checks. I was so grateful to my boss, she knew my current situation with Andrew, and I think she put my need to be busy down to that. I had never told anyone about Steve, but Janice.

I was gradually building up my savings, and I applied for a credit card. I was sure that I would have to rely on something to help us get by at some point. I also began looking for a new place for us all to stay. I had it narrowed down to two potential flats, however, the first one preferred to have an older couple, and no children. The other one was more for students, as it meant sharing a kitchen, and a bathroom. Both were fairly cheap but no good. So I carried on scanning the papers every day.

One evening there was a private message for me on the site, and so I logged on. My heart began beating furiously, and I felt a little bit light headed when I saw who it was from I was sad, because it wan't Steve.

I opened up the message, and it was from a new user "ilovemy-kids" and it was one of those chat up messages. He was trying to lure me into a conversation about dating, saying he was single with kid's blah, blah...

I had a deep suspicion that it was Andrew. Did he think I was really that stupid? He had created an account to see what I was getting up to. He must have sensed or seen the change in me up until a few weeks ago, and known there was maybe someone else. I began to feel as if my stomach had dropped, and then a wave of nausea hit me.

I messaged Louise, and she promptly banned him. Afterward, she messaged me to show me his registration email, and it was, in fact, Andrew's.

I studied Andrew that night, and there was nothing about him that gave himself away. He was courteous and did his usual... spend time with the children, eat dinner, and then out with whoever it was that he was seeing.

∞∞∞∞

A little later on I got another private message, and my heart started thudding all over again because this time the message was from Steve.

He had heard that Andrew had created an account from Louise, and he was concerned and wanted to make sure I was okay and to tell me the offer of a place to stay was still open. I thanked him, but knowing deep down that I could never move three hundred miles away, and have the children never seeing their Grandparents, or their father. It would be selfish, and unfair. I thought.

Deep down though I wanted nothing more than to run to Steve, to be with him, and to see him every day, not because I needed him, but because I wanted him... I loved him. Which reminded me again... that it was because of my love for him that I would not put him through any of this. This was my problem, I needed to deal with it, and I was almost ready to start a fresh new life with the children, and certainly no Andrew!

∞∞∞∞

I realized after having the conversation with Steve that it was a little easier talking to him sometimes, rather than not at all. I had tried to go sort of go cold turkey, but I just didn't have the will power.

Chapter Seventy One

Heavenly Mountains

J anice was glaring at me. "Why not?!" she snapped.

"Because too many things's could go wrong, what if he finds out and takes the children away with him, to his parents? I have no one, Janice, there is no one to help me in that situation!"

"He wouldn't do that, he will try to force you back, the same as he's always done, and if he does find out you went to Visit Steve and takes the kid's then you have police reports, a Doctors report."

"Janice I told the Doctor that I fell, that it was an accident. As for the police, the neighbors called but Andrew always told them we were just arguing, I didn't dare say anything else, imagine if I had? I probably wouldn't be sitting here today!"

"No, but neither would he then, would he? You called them to though didn't you?"

"I went to them one time because he had all my things, and I had nowhere to go. All they did was ask him firmly to open the door and let me in to get my thing's."

"Keith and I will protect you I promise. Look, Evie, when are you going to live your life for you? When are going to let yourself enjoy being in love? You are my best friend, and I am yours and I'm telling you to go! Your children will be fine, you have already told Andrew that I'm having the kids during the days on the weekends. I will go on about how much I really wanted to go on this paranormal weekend trip with you, and you! Will go and have a bloody good time!"

"I'm scared Janice. I don't like all the lying, and I've never been away from both of the children for three whole nights."

"They will be just fine. You know they will. He loves those kid's, but I know damn well and so do you, and that no matter what you do he will always try to use them as his leverage. That 's the only reason why he has agreed to you going you know? and that is because he has them, and you won't, so he knows that you are coming back."

"I don't understand why he just won't let me move on. He knows we are finished, he hasn't tried anything with me physically, except trying to spy, or catch me out by private messaging me under a username. If he has someone new, which I'm sure he does, then why doesn't he just leave?"

"Because you are letting him stay. Did you ask him to leave?"

"No, but only because his name is on the lease. It would have to be me."

"Exactly, and he knows you can't leave the flat right now. I think he is just biding his time with you,"

"What do you mean exactly?"

He's either going to try and get you to stay at the last minute, by maybe threatening or hurting you, or.... he's going to manipulate you somehow."

"Well, it won't work. I almost have enough saved now. I was thinking about getting a restraining order. When I leave"

"Look why don't you just leave now. We can find space for you and the kid's, and take it from there."

"No Janice I can't do that. He would make yours and Keith's lives a misery. I couldn't do that to you both. I will be okay. I just need a couple more weeks, and I will take whatever property I can get, and... I will go to see Steve, and well we will have to see. " I grinned with renewed grit and determination, but I still wasn't completely without fear.

∞∞∞

I kissed my beautiful children goodbye. I told them how much I loved them, and that I would call them every day. I said goodbye to Andrew, and as I walked away with my small suitcase I heard him say...

"I will miss you too. Call me."

I boarded the train at Brighton train station. I had to change at London Victoria, and from there I took a train to Carlisle.

Steve rang me several times on my journey, checking that I was okay, and all the trains were on time.

We both had butterflies in our tummies. I had lost a couple of stone in the space of a couple of a couple of months. Neither of us had been really able to eat anything much. We were definitely both very lovesick.

As the train continued to roll forwards, ever closer towards my best friend, and my love, I was gripped with a myriad of emotions, switching between love, panic, excitement, and fear.

I don't know exactly where I was when I looked out of the train window when I saw two beautiful, and enormous dark grey, mossy mountains side by side. I couldn't see the top of them for they were hidden by clouds. I also noticed a very long sloped waterfall between them.

This is heaven I thought, with a slight gasp. I sat upright, leaning closer till my nose was almost touching the window.

Gone were motorways, gone were fields of green, gone were Smokey buildings, and the high rises, this... was something else! This was... the Lake District!

The land was no longer flat; it was all craggy hills, and old stone cottages with slate roofs, farmhouses, brooks, and Lakes. Everywhere looked so clean and so clear. If there was a heaven, to me this was the place.

My phone rang, and it was Steve. I described where I was, which was Oxenholme near Kendal, according to Steve.

"You're only roughly about thirty minutes away!" he gushed excitedly.

I asked him if where he lived was anything like Kendal, and he replied...

"Yes, it's all pretty much the same."

When we each hung up, knowing that the next time we spoke, it would be face to face.

Chapter Seventy-Two

Peace

The train came to a screeching halt. I looked out of my window at the large busy platform. People were rushing backward and forwards in the Friday late afternoon rush hour. I stood up, and pulled the handle up on my suitcase, steeled my nerves by taking in a deep breath, and made my way to the exit door of the carriage.

I stepped down and scanned the length of the platform. There were bright colored sprays of flowers hanging from baskets along the platform. I noticed several doors, which were the toilets and probably storerooms, but I couldn't see Steve. There were several people in front of me as well as behind, and so I had to keep on walking towards the exit. But then I saw him, and he looked at me. We both grinned, then shouted each other's names, waving frantically. I began to run a little, and when I was within feet of him he opened out his arms, and I ran into them, closed my eyes and at the exact same time we both whispered: "I love you."

Steve put my case in the boot of his silver Corsa breeze, whom he called Gale, and opened the car door for me. I had never had anyone open a car door for me, ever. On the drive to his home, we held hands, and all the way back were repeatedly taking glances at each other, and smiling every time. He lifted our joined hands a few times, to kiss my hand.

∞∞∞∞

We spent that weekend visiting his family. Everyone was so down to earth and very kind. I loved their Cumbrian accents. They kept calling me lass, it was endearing. God only knows what my accent sounded like to them. I must have sounded like the bloody queen of England, comparing my words to their richly rugged ones. I learned that in the village in which they lived, everyone seemed to know everyone, and everyone's grandparents, and great-grandparents. Kid's played out in the streets, and everyone was sitting in their front gardens watching them all. I felt as if I had stepped into another world, in another time.

Steve's and his family seemed to enjoy their light-hearted teasing of each other, and they were a case of what she saw is what you got, and I really loved that about all of them.

They were so different from Andrew and the rest of his family. They all seemed a bit straight-laced, compared to Steve's family. I felt as if I didn't have to mind what I said or did, and they made me feel well, comfortable, and free to be me.

∞∞∞∞

Steve and I sat cozily together on his living room sofa with a Chinese takeaway and we watched "Days Of Thunder", by candlelight. If anyone were to ever ask me what my perfect date night was, it would have been something like this, or by a lake with a cozy campfire underneath a blanket of stars, with Steve, away from the world, and all life's problems.

We talked, laughed, kissed and cuddled. This I thought is how it really felt to be in love, and I felt so incredibly lucky. The only thing I could have asked for to make it completely perfect was the children.

I called them as promised every day, and Janice too. Andrew tried to keep me on the phone a few times. Steve was great though. He would place a hand on my shoulder gently, and mouth he would give me some space, and told me to do or discuss whatever I needed to. Afterward, Steve would ask how the children were, and just hold me. He knew how much I missed them, and how painful it was being so far away from them.

The first time we made love was on the second night. Once I had gotten over my initial nerves it was easy and wonderful. Steve was slow, and there was so much love in every kiss or caress. He whispered how much he loved me, and we were able to look into each other's eyes. I wasn't like some scripted hot lovers scene, that you see in the movies, well... if it was, it was ours. I didn't think once about hiding under a t-shirt or about hiding myself in general. I felt completely natural, and... loved.

Chapter Seventy-Three

My Decision

I t was painful for us both having to say goodbye on the train platform. If it wasn't for my children I would have stayed there with him in bliss forever. It was time to go back to the real world. It was like reading a romance novel when it starts to get really good, and then something snaps you back into reality, and you have to put the book away, knowing that as soon as you are free again, you will go right back to where you were in the book. That's kind of how it felt.

We kissed each other with tears in our eyes, our hearts heavy, but hopeful as we had a plan, and I was going to follow through with it no matter the cost to my body, or emotions. Andrew was going to let me go.

I placed my suitcase in the living room beside my futon bed. I hugged and kissed the children like I hadn't seen them for months. I played with them for a while, bathed them and put them to sleep, kissing them both on the soft warm cheeks.

I looked at my little boy, now four years old and I said to him...

"No matter what you hear, you go to sleep okay? If you hear loud noises it is okay. Mummy loves you. You stay here with your little sister. Promise me?"

Caleb nodded, and I kissed both of them once more.

I closed their door and went into the living room where Andrew was seated, and I closed the door behind me, shutting us both in.

∞∞∞

I had to be brave. I had to be strong. I know what love is now, and this situation has to stop. I repeated it over and over in my head like a mantra.

"Andrew we need to talk," I said as firmly as I could muster because of no matter what I had to appear unafraid. If he thought I was or showed it he would see it as a weakness, and try to intimidate me.

Andrew turned off the TV and turned to face me. He knew something was coming, it was written all over his face. I could see the muscle in his jaw twitching, which meant his teeth were clamped.

"I've had a lot of time to think over the weekend Andrew, and I think that it is time that we both moved on. The way we are living is not good for either of us, and it will only confuse the children in the long run." I spoke as calmly, and as slowly as I could, without falter.

"I knew you going away was a bad idea," he said darkly, staring down at the floor. "So which one of your new friends has been filling your head with crap?" he asked trying to stare me down.

I could feel his anger bubbling up beneath the surface of his stony stare.

"No one. I've been thinking about it for a while. Don't you want to be free to move on? I want to be happy too Andrew. I don't want the children to see us like this, it's not fair. I know you know that what I am saying is right, even if you don't want to agree with me." I said it softly, with as much feeling as I could muster, because what I really wanted to tell him was to get the hell out of my life.

Andrew got up abruptly, making me flinch, but not enough to make him notice. I watched as he walked the length of the living room, before coming to a standstill in front of me.

"Do you love me, at all?" he asked slowly.

I looked him in the eye, my body now tense. "No, I don't. I haven't for a long time Andrew, and I know you do not love me either."

I watched him carefully and I stood for what felt like a long time, until he looked at me, his bottom lip quivering as if he was going to cry.

"Have you got someone else?" he asked.

I know he was hoping I would say no, and it would probably have made my life a lot easier if I had of said no. I was going to say no, but I surprised myself when I said...

"Yes. I have." I said confidently, and I pictured Steve's loving face. "Andrew I think it is best if you stay with your parents for a day or two, just to give me a chance to get mine and the children's things together, so we can move into a place of our own." I could see that he was about to protest, but I quickly interrupted him "I promise that I won't be far, and you are welcome to see the children whenever you like. They are your children and I won't ever try to stop you. I would never do that. If you won't go then I will have to go with the children, today."

I expected Andrew to get angry, to shout or try to break me down in some way, but instead, he walked out of the living room, and into his room.

I was too scared to sleep that night because his reaction to walk away was completely out of character. I really didn't know what it meant either. Was he going to leave like I asked or was he going to leave it for me to leave him? The only thing I could do was wait.

∞∞∞

The next morning Andrew was dressed in his paint-splattered work clothes, and in his hand was a large black suitcase." I will collect the rest of my things tonight."

"O okay." I stuttered. "Just come back to get them whenever you are ready, and you can see the children as well for a bit." I tried to say it offhandily...But I don't think I managed to pull it off as confidently as I had hoped.

I was very surprised that he still hadn't said or done anything to me. His silence and compliance were more worrying to me that it would be if he had of thrown me across the room.

Chapter Seventy Four

A lioness And Her Cubs

I didn't say anything to the children about their father, instead, I got Caleb ready for school, and Holly ready for nursery. I gave them their cereal and morning juice, and then I dropped them both off. I told each class teacher that no one was to collect the children but me. I was feeling really uneasy. I didn't know why, but I wanted to protect the children. I then went to work.

I explained the situation to my boss, and she was happy for me to bring both of the children to work with me, and they could play or whatever in the back of the shop. From 5 pm, until 8 pm, so I wasn't giving up my hours, because I needed them now more than ever.

I called Steve at lunchtime, he was pleased that Andrew had agreed to leave without a fuss, but like me, he thought I should be very careful. Steve suggested that I go and stay with Janice and Keith that night. I decided to wait and see.

When I got home from work the TV in the living room had gone, as well as the computer and the rest of his personal belongings. I didn't expect him to come back again later on, but he did.

"I'm taking the children to see my mum and Dad for a little

while." He announced whilst trying to put their coats on.

"Okay, but Andrew I need them home in time for their dinner, and baths?" I said, feeling very concerned, but what could I do? His demeanor and abruptness just did not feel right at all.

Two hours went by and I had heard nothing. I decided to call Andrews mobile, and it just rang and rang. It wasn't until my third attempt that he answered the phone.

"Andrew, thank god. Where are you? I've been worried."

My chest felt tight, and I was struggling to breathe evenly. I wanted the children back so badly, but I was trying to remain calm.

"The children are staying with me at mum and dads. You're not getting them back!" he shouted at me down the phone, but I could tell he was driving and I could hear Holly crying in the back, and I could also hear Caleb's muffled voice, probably trying to comfort her.

"Andrew please bring the children back right this minute, or I will call the police!" I snapped at him, and then I heard a beep, and he had hung up on me.

NO! NO! I shouted.

I quickly tried to dial his parent's house number. I felt really light headed, and I was finding it difficult to breathe through my sobs and panic. My mind felt as if it was racing a hundred miles an hour. After a few short rings, his mother answered.

"Please it's Evie Andrew is refusing to bring the children back home, and he's driving around somewhere with them, and I could hear Holly crying."

"Calm down. Andrew will bring them back."

"NO! He is not bringing them back. Please call him and tell him to bring them back or I will call the police. I mean it." And I slammed the phone down.

I waited, and waited, pacing the living room back and forth. I just could not imagine not being with the children, and certainly not leaving them with him! Who would care for them? Everyone worked.

I decided to call Steve and when I heard the sound of his voice all I could do was sob aloud that "He took the children! Oh my god, he took my children!"

∞∞∞

Steve managed to calm me just enough to try and stay focused. He told me that I needed to call the police and make a statement about everything he had done and ask them to help me get them back. Steve was also trying to ready himself to drive all the way from the Lake District to East Sussex, which would have been a seven to eight-hour drive.

"No Steve you had better not. I don't want you mixed up in all of this. I have Janice and Keith they will help me. Please just stay and I will call you to let you know what's going on. He's not taking the children. I won't let him."

Steve left me with some strong comforting words, and then I hung up. I took several deep breaths, trying to calm myself because I knew if I did it straight away then I would sound like a crazed woman and as Steve had said it would not help.

∞∞∞

When I was ready I dialed 999 for the police, as an emergency. I managed to remain calm, and reasonable, and I explained very slowly the situation, and they promised to send two officers immediately.

Two uniformed policemen arrived at the flat within less than ten minutes. I explained that I had been subjected to domestic violence for many years and that I had finally gotten the courage to ask him to leave. I explained that I was not stopping him from seeing his children, but that I would like them to remain with me.

I managed to explain everything calmly, and I tried very hard not to cry. I had to show them I was reasonable and not as crazed as I felt in my mind.

The police officers were disgusted at hearing about his treatment of me, though they explained they could do nothing, without evidence. I explained again that I just wanted my children so I could take care of them, and I was happy to just leave it at that if they could get him to bring them back.

One of the police officers agreed that that was fair and called Andrew on his mobile. The officer told Andrew to bring them back, or he would risk facing other charges and arrest. I could hear Andrew yelling at the officer, but I couldn't make out what exactly it was that he was saying. The officer then asked Andrew if he was using a hands-free kit, whilst driving. I knew Andrew didn't use one, and I knew where the officer was going with his question.

∞∞∞

Andrew brought the children back about ten minutes later. The officers took Andrew outside and they closed the front door too. I hugged the children, still trying not to cry I didn't want to upset them with my tears. I sent them off to their room to play with their toys, and I promised them that I would be back.

It was a good ten to fifteen minutes later before the officers lightly tapped on the front door, asking if they could re-enter, to which I told them to please come in, and I thanked them both.

He's trouble that one. I think you are doing the right thing. I can't technically order him away from the property, as his name is on the lease to this flat. But what I have done is ask him to relinquish his key to the property and to stay away from the property for a few days, to give you a chance to make your plans. I will put a note on the system. The only way we could keep him away was by letting him off with driving whilst using a mobile. If he does come back and not honor the agreement then I will make sure that he face's prosecution for that. I also explained that he faces other potential charges such as GBH (grievous bodily harm) if he was to hurt you again. He wasn't a happy chap, but he agreed.

"Oh thank you! Thank you so much. I am very grateful to you both." I said with so much relief. "Has he gone now?"

"Yes and here is his front door key. If you get any more trouble you can call us, and he wrote down the station number along with his extension, name and badge number."

I didn't call Steve until I had fed the children and then settled them down for the night.

I apologized to him for my frantic call and thanked him for trying to get me to stay calm whilst dealing with the police. He was right If I'd have called them up shrieking, and crying I wasn't going to appear stable enough to get the children back. By my calmness and Andrew's anger, I came off much better in that situation. In a situation like that, it is important to try and stay as calm, and reasonable as you possibly can.

Andrew called me a couple of days later to tell me that I

could transfer the lease into my own name, and he said that he would not come back until the five days was up and then it would only be to see the children. I agreed.

I spent the next two days sorting out the new tenancy agreement, and all I had to do was wait for the paperwork, sign it and send it back, as the people that owned the shopping center, also owned the flats, and they were based in London or somewhere like that.

Chapter Seventy-Five

Relentless

The following weekend Steve had made plans with me, to come and stay with us for the weekend. I thought that it was a good idea for the children to meet him. Especially, before I decided to take them to the Lake District. I thought that it would be better for him to meet them in their own surroundings. I was excited, as I wanted him to meet them, but I was also worried that they would be confused or upset with me sharing my attention with someone that they didn't know.

We both decided that it was best if we kept our affections as low key as possible in front of them, though we worried needlessly, as Caleb took to Steve straight away. In fact, Caleb followed Steve wherever he went with a cheeky grin. Holly was a little more reserved and slower to come forward, but we just let her be and thought that she would make up her mind when she was ready.

That first Friday night after I had put the children to bed Steve and I snuggled down on the futon in the living room, and we set an alarm for early the following morning so that we wouldn't get caught out before they awoke in the morning.

∞∞∞

It was very strange having Steve in the flat, let alone even having him in my bed of sorts. There were so many negative memories there, and I wasn't feeling completely comfortable beginning a new life with all of those memories. I decided that I wasn't going to sign the new lease. I was going to get a new flat. There was one going across the road from the community center on the opposite side of the road. The kids would lose their garden roof, but I would take them to the park as often as I could on nice days. Yes, I thought... I would do it on Monday.

I got a phone call from Liz, and she was asking us if Steve and I would like to join her and her family for a social get together, so she too could meet Steve. We agreed, and we packed a few things for me, and the children. Steve took some things from his case, putting them in mine, and then we set off by train.

∞∞∞

Liz and her husband got on really well with Steve. We all ate dinner together, and her two boys played in their back garden with my two, leaving us adults to relax and discuss all of our plans for the rest of the summer.

Liz a little, later on, took me into the kitchen to talk about Andrew. She said she didn't want to tell me before because she was worried that I either wouldn't believe her, or be mad at her now for not saying, but that she needed to tell me now...

Liz told me that Andrew had called her on messenger with his webcam on, and apparently, he was stark naked. Colin her husband had come home from work and saw him, just before Andrew noticed him and then he quickly ended the video call.

I wouldn't say I was surprised or shocked, more embarrassed that he had done this to her.

" I think he did it, hoping that you wouldn't speak or see me again Liz. I'm sorry he did that."

"Oh no don't be. I thought it was quite funny really, he was acting like some cheap porn actor." And she laughed.

"Liz!?" her husband called from the living room. A message has popped up to you from Evie's messenger."

"What?" I exclaimed. I've been hacked?"

It was Andrew on my messenger account, telling Liz to get me to call him. I remember thinking how the heck did he know where I was?

Of course, I called him though. I wanted to know how he knew where I was and how he had got onto my account.

Andrew was begging me to go back to him. He said to me...

"I know Steve is there with you and the children, and I know that you have slept together. I have washed your bed sheets, and if you come back to me we will just forget all about it."

I was absolutely flabbergasted! Seve and I had actually done anything but sleep that night, as he was exhausted from the drive, and how on earth did he know Steve's name? I had his key, and I never saw his car anywhere.

I asked him, but he wouldn't tell me how he managed to get into the flat without a key. I decided to hang up the phone, and I thought about calling the police, but then Liz's house phone began ringing... it was Andrew again.

Liz had told him to cease calling, and in the end, they had to unplug their house phone because he called them more than ten times. Andrew was then unable to call their house, he began using my account to message Liz. Liz, in the end, had to block my account.

I was so mortified, and I lost count the number of times that I apologized to them, despite them telling me that it wasn't my fault. They thought Andrew was completely crazy.

I tucked the children into bed in a spare bedroom, and Colin had set up a blow-up bed for Steve and me in the living room.

Liz and Colin were both glad that Steve and I were with them, and they really didn't want us to go anywhere.

Andrew hadn't wanted me for years, and he had said himself so many times that he was only with me because of the children. I had never asked Andrew to stay, and I had wanted to be free of him for so long. I think he realized then that he had lost his control over me and he was desperately trying to get it back, and so far he was failing, and I was afraid.

∞∞∞

Poor Steve I really thought that this wonderful, amazing guy is not going to be able to put up with all this. I was feeling really mortified.

I was also scared too because somehow Andrew he had managed to get inside the flat, which meant that he was probably there right now, and tomorrow he would probably refuse to go.

I found it very strange that he had said that he had washed the sheets that Steve and I had slept on. Did it mean that he had actually examined them to see if we had done anything?

∞∞∞

Steve cuddled me up and promised me that he wasn't going anywhere, despite me telling him that it was Okay, and I understood if he didn't want to be with me.

"I love you, and your kids are amazing. Evie, I wish you would let me call him or see him I would just love to put him in his place." He said frustratedly.

"No Steve please, I don't want you involved in all of this."

"Look you are not alone anymore. You have me and I will bloody well keep him in his place. He can hit a woman, well I would like to see him try having a crack at me because he won't manage it." Steve said hotly.

I giggled." I know you would., but your better than him, by far! and I don't want you to do anything because he is still the father of my children, and besides I don't want him to start saying things about you. He can be very cruel Steve. He really does have problems, but he won't get help. He likes to blame other people for everything that goes wrong in his life. He doesn't like to take responsibility for his wrong doing's. He's mean, but he also has this charming side and sadly that's the one that most people see." I gave a long sigh, and I wrapped myself tighter against Steve. "Thank you for coming into my life. I do love you, very, very much. I feel safe with you."

Steve suddenly got up. "I'll be right back, do not go anywhere, and stay right there. Okay?" he grinned.

"Uh okay. I promise." I replied, wondering what on earth he was up to.

Steve was gone for about ten minutes. I heard him talking to Liz and Colin, and then I heard them in the kitchen. After a few more minutes had passed Liz and Colin entered into the living room grinning.

"Steve wants you in the kitchen." Said Liz with a huge smile.

"In the kitchen... Whatever for?" I asked frowning in puzzlement.

"There is more room, just go and see!" she was grinning like a

Cheshire cat.

Slowly I made my way apprehensively to the kitchen. At the doorway, I noticed the warm glowing of candles, and Steve was standing in the center of the room.

"Evie. This isn't how I ever imagined that I would do this, and I know that this is ridiculously too soon. But I love you, and I want to take care of you and the children. I can't bear it when we are apart, and I don't ever want to be apart from you again. Please be my wife... will you marry me?"

Steve got down on one knee right beside the kitchen bin, he saw me looking at the bin, and he took a candle off the worktop, placed it on top of the metal lid, and got back down on one knee again. In his hand was a ring, with blue diamonds.

I could not believe it! He was asking me to marry him? I was still bloody married I thought, and the kid's had only just met him. I sensed Liz and her Colin behind us.

"Go on Evie... it's not as if you have both just met!"

"Shh," Colin said to her, as he too was waiting for my answer.

How on earth are we going to do this? I remember thinking, as I knelt down in front of him, threw my arms around his neck, and kissed him passionately.

"Yes. I will marry you."

Liz exclaimed in excitement, and Colin patted Steve on the shoulder exchanging some words, whilst Liz hugged me tightly.

"The ring was my grandmother's, it's on loan until he buys you one that will fit." She whispered and kissed my cheek.

Chapter Seventy-Six

Swept Away

"I want you and the children to come back with me. I don't want you going back to that flat, and I don't want Andrew anywhere near you. You are mine now, to care for and love, and I won't have you in harm's way." He kissed me deeply.

"What about the children's school and nursery, their friends. It means They won't be able to see their father?"

They will have new schools. I'm sure they will love it, and they will have lots of new friends. If you want to work, then you can, when you are ready. As for Andrew he can come and see them or we can bring them."

"I will ask Caleb, and try to explain to Holly, though I don't think they will really understand."

"You will all have my family too, don't forget that, we always look out for our own, you included."

"Oh Steve what will they think about us getting engaged, whilst I'm still married, and taking off to live with you only after meeting you in person a week ago!" I smiled painstakingly.

"They won't bother, as long as I'm happy, which I am. I am very happy. You will be fine. I promise you."

"Steve?"

"Yes?"

"How on earth am I going to move with you in your little car, with two children and a butt load of cases?"

"Ahh I've already called my mam and step-dad Joe, they are on their way down with my uncle and his transit van."

I could feel the blood rushing in my ears. Oh my! This is all happening so fast. One minute he is here to meet the children, and the next I've agreed to marry him and move in with him, all in the space of nearly two days.

"We are crazy Steve!" I gasped.

"Crazy in love" he replied, kissing me again.

The next morning we set off back on the train, to pack up mine and the children's belongings, and I got to thinking.

Andrew had asked me to get engaged, whilst he was still married to Beth. What was I doing? But then after I had thought about it I came to the conclusion that both situations were very different because unlike me Steve knew the situation, whereas I did not when he was still married to Beth. I was also in love and ready to be loved, it was my time. It felt right.

I don't think I could ever have said No to Steve. Deep down. Over the past year there was hardly a day that went by when we didn't talk. We each knew others thoughts and secrets and like Janice he was my best friend. I didn't know how it was ever going to tun out, but I knew one thing... I wanted to find out. I had never imagined I could feel so in love, or be loved so much by any man. But then Steve wasn't just any man... he was my man. I smiled.

∞∞∞∞

The plan was to wait for his parents, and uncle to arrive, and they would wait for us in the car park in case there was any trouble, or if Andrew was to turn up.

Andrew's mum Jane accompanied me and the children up to the flat. My hand was shaking as I put the key in the lock to open it. His mum waited out on the balcony, as an extra pair of eyes and I sent the children to their rooms to help me pack.

I managed to pack all of their clothes, toys, coats, and shoes, and I was left with black sacks. I began putting my clothes into a sack when I heard a car screeching in the car park.

I took some toys out of a bag and told the children to stay in the room, and I closed the door.

I then heard Andrew shouting something angrily. I decided to just grab what I could and leave it. I was panicking about Steve and his father, and uncle. I didn't want there to be any trouble. I was shaking so hard. All I could do now was wait, and confront him.

"You were going to leave, and sneak off?" he shouted, advancing on me.

Andrew brought his head back. I knew he was going to head butt me, but there was a sound, and he was distracted, and so was I.

Steves mum Jane was standing clear in the doorway, and she alerted to her presence by clearing her throat. God bless her. I thought. She was one brave woman. Andrew must have been so angry that he didn't see her standing off to the side.

I don't remember everything he said, but I do remember getting the children and letting him say goodbye. Steve's mum took their little hands and distracted them by chatting to them all the way down to the car park, and the waiting men.

I didn't speak, and I didn't look back.

∞∞∞

When I got to the car park I noticed the caretaker, whom I'd always thought of as rather creepy, and I knew that he was the one to let Andrew in, and when I thought about it, the kitchen window was open with the rubber hanging off, and that was how he broke in.

I kissed the children and put them in the van with their belongings, and I turned to Steve.

"He knew your name because when he was in the flat, he went through your suitcase. Are you all okay?"

"Of course we are." Piped up Steve's step-father Joe, whom if I haven't said before now is a cheeky Scotsman with a big heart, but did not suffer fools gladly.

"He would have had a hard job starting anything with us." He laughed, his uncle agreed.

"They aren't joking," Steve said nodding in their direction.

Steve and I held onto each other for a short while, before we began our long journey to the Lake District.

∞∞∞

I got in the van with Steves uncle and his step-father. I sat in the back with the kid's, and my half a black sack of clothes, god knows what I put in there, probably nothing useful!. I felt a bit like little orphan Annie. The children were smiling like this was some sort of big, strange adventure.

Steve drove his little car Gale, with his mum sat beside him.

We stopped several times on the way back. However all the way I expected Andrew to be following, or to have called the police, and so I then envisioned a police car chasing us too. My nerves felt like they were shot to pieces, and everyone else seemed calm and positive.

Chapter Seventy-Seven

Traveling a road a little less broken

I do believe that each one of them saved my life that day because God only knows what could have happened to me if I had been alone in that flat when Andrew came back.

∞∞∞

When we arrived at Steve's house, the children ran from room to room, exploring their new surroundings. They each chose a room of their own, and Steve and I helped them to settle in, by unpacking all of their belongings and folding them neatly with their separate drawers. Steve ran me a bath. I felt quite bad as he had driven for seven hours, yet still, he insisted on me taking a bubble bath, whilst he helped the children. This all felt so unreal to me, but so wonderful, and scary all at the same time.

I remember lying in the bath and listening to the children squealing in delight, at Steve who was making them laugh by putting on silly voices, and pretending to hurt himself. Children always seem to find it funny when you hurt yourself don't they? I loved their laughter.

After we had all freshened up Steve cooked us all homemade spaghetti bolognese, and it was delicious!

Because it was the children's first night so far away from every-thing that they knew, and in strange new bedrooms I lay with each child, stroking their hair until they fell asleep.

My first night with Steve felt almost surreal, more so because the children were actually there with us when a week ago I had dreamed that one day it may have become a possibility. I never expected it to be this soon though, and neither did Steve, but we were all so very happy. I fell asleep that night snuggled deeply within Steve's embrace.

∞∞∞

The next day we found out that Andrew had been calling his uncles house impersonating as a policeman in a bid to gain information from Steve's auntie. We came to the conclusion that Andrew had got the number from Steve's suitcase, that he left at the flat. The case had previously belonged to his uncle and had their phone number on the case's tag.

Thankfully he wasn't very convincing, and that was the end of that.

Over the next few days, Steve helped us to get registered with a Doctor, as well as a Dentist, and Steve came with me to look around a few of the local schools, and we eventually enrolled Caleb in a lovely, small primary school, and Holly into the nursery, also attached to the school. They were to begin after the summer holidays.

Steve's mum Jane and I went shopping for some clothes, as I hadn't managed to bring anything of great use with me in the half-filled sack, not even a coat.

Steve called Andrew and gave him our home number, as well as an email address to communicate. Andrew was quite nasty with Steve, but it didn't faze him in the slightest, he was straight to the point and very firm. Steve told him that if he wanted to talk to the kid's he could in the evenings, and if he had anything to ask me or wanted to speak to me about anything, then he was to use the email address Steve provided.

∞∞∞

The children kept in touch with their grandparents, calling them two to three times a week. Andrew ended up only calling them once a week, on a Saturday.

I found myself a really good family solicitor and filed for divorce. Andrew refused to sign the papers, and so Jane told me to call his bluff, and play him at his own silly games, and so I did. I told him that I couldn't care less if he divorced me or not, and at the end of the day, I was safe and very happily in love. I had everything I needed which was the children, and Steve, so I could wait out the five years of separation before being granted a divorce by the court.

∞∞∞

Andrew did eventually angrily agree to a divorce, and later confessed to being in a relationship with a nursery school assistant, and I managed to get him to admit to adultery with an unnamed woman as I agreed to protect her name. The solicitor recommended that I go for a private maintenance agreement, where he was to pay fifty pounds a week, for both children. It meant that I wouldn't have to go through a third party agency, and it also meant that if he didn't pay then he would be taken to court instead.

Andrew agreed and signed the papers.

I was divorced within two months.

Chapter Seventy-Nine

Closure ... or not?

I explained to Steve all about my past once we were settled. I told him about Melvin sexually abusing me, about Derek's physically, and emotionally abusing me, and of course all about my mother, and Lucy. I explained to him that it had been four years since I had seen or spoken with my mother, because of Andrew, and a little over two years since I had seen or spoken to Lucy.

∞∞∞∞

The last time that I saw Lucy was a couple of years before when she asked me about what had happened to me when I was younger with Melvin, and why I left her? I had never, ever discussed anything with her before, mainly because I didn't want to taint her with my memories, and how on earth could I tell her that Melvin was beginning to look at her in the same way that he did me? I knew in my heart, that he was going to do to Lucy, what he had done to me for years. I saw the way his eyes followed her, and he told me once that he was going to love her, just like he loved me. He even asked me if I thought she could keep the same secret. I said no, and I wanted him to be afraid of that.

I chose instead... to briefly explain what Melvin had done to me, and that was why I was sent away. I never mentioned what Derek had done because he was her father, and she loved him. It was enough for me that My mother knew. There was another reason and that was because of the time that I had briefly moved back in with Derek and Lucy to help out. During that brief period, I did get to see a softer side of him. He was still grumpy, old fashioned and set in his ways. He was still very abrupt, and at times very rude, but I did find a peace with him... for my mother and Lucy. I didn't feel that I had much of a choice really, not if I wanted to keep them in my life you see.

Anyway, Lucy went off and questioned our mother, who was still apparently living with Derek, and then later she called me to tell me that my mother had said it was all lies. After the telephone call with Lucy, we ceased speaking.

I felt as if there was nothing I could do or say to anyone. What would happen? Probably nothing, and so I gave up trying.

After I had explained everything to Steve, I said that I was still angry inside, but sad, because my mother had never seen her grandchildren, and I was still left with no closure. I now saw my mother as someone who had let these men commit these terrible wrongs to me and gave them her full support, all for the sake of her own selfish needs. I hated to think like that because despite all of that I still loved her. I can't explain why. I don't know why. I also didn't want to live my life never knowing if she was sick, or had passed away.

Now living in the Lake District I felt even farther away from them. In truth...I missed them, and I know that may seem utterly crazy! But I did. I wished I didn't feel that way, but that is exactly how I felt at the time. All I ever wanted was to love, and have the love of my mother and for her to be truly and openly sorry for what she put me through as a child, and to stand up for my truth. Could she ever? I wondered.

∞ ∞ ∞

Should I try? I asked Steve, or should I just get on with my life and try to not think of them again? Steve is a very open and honest kind of a guy, however, and he said that

"It is hard to judge what you should do, or what anyone should do after experiencing everything that you have. I can give you my honest opinion on what I think you should do, but then I could be swaying you. The truth is darling, I can't tell you, but it's got to be your choice. No matter what you decide though I will be there to support you, and I will always, always be there for you and the kid's."

I understood what he was saying, but I needed him to tell me what he thought. The fact that he didn't, told me that he would not be trying to contact her, but at the same time, he was telling me I could, and He would be there. I hung on to that thought..."No matter what you decide though I will be there to support you"

With that... I chose to call her, and I dialed their house number.

Chapter Eighty

Tying to forgive

My mother with no surprise was still with Derek, despite them getting a divorce, years before. They, in fact, had been planning on re-marrying, and Lucy was now engaged to be married.

My mother had spent several moments crying and was shocked that I was now living in the North of the country. My mother had begun to tell me how much she had missed me and asked me about the children.

After a little bit of small talk, she did, in fact, apologize to me, for telling Lucy that it wasn't true about what had happened to me because she was so hurt and angry that I had hadn't spoken to her for two years before all that with Lucy.

I explained that Andrew would not let me have anything to do with her and that he threatened to do something to her, and me if I ever tried. I didn't know whether Andrew would have tried to do anything her or not, but I knew he would have to me.

"It was wrong, and I should never have said what I said. I'm so sorry." She repeated again.

My mother did explain to me why she had betrayed me when I was younger, and again when Lucy approached her, and she said in all honesty that it was because, without Derek, she had nothing. She said to me that if she had of shown me her support, then she knew that it would have upset him, and she didn't have had anywhere else to go, despite her having relatives living close by. When I did ask her why could she not just go and stay with them? Her response was that their homes were already too overcrowded, and she didn't want to live like that. My mother had made it sound as if she had no other choice, but to let me go. After that, she then cried calling herself a terrible mother for all of her drinking, and neglect of me.

∞∞∞

I remember feeling as if I was at a stalemate. I was torn. My instinct was telling me to put the phone down, but I couldn't do it. I would later wish that I had put the phone down, but hindsight is a wonderful thing... and I went with the other option... I would try my very best to forgive her.

My mother asked to see me, Steve and the children. I agreed and that's what we did. The more we talked the more I began to find a peace with her too, and I think now it was because I felt sorry for her, you see she had lost an awful lot of weight. I think she had gone from a size sixteen, down to a size eight. It was primarily down to her being an alcoholic, but also because she had some health problems with her chest and things. I could physically see that she was no longer a strong person, and she was a little more meek in nature. I could see that without Derek that she would struggle, as she was not the sort of person to want to live alone, and even though she was working and had her wages, that sometimes it was not enough to cover her alcohol and cigarettes. To be honest I felt that one life (mine) had been almost ruined, and now what was the point in hers being ruined also, over something that could never be changed or taken away?

I knew that I was probably much too soft, and possibly very

silly, but I didn't want to see it. I don't think in truth that anyone could have told me not to see her, even by someone reminding me of everything. My choices were to close everyone off or forgive, and I just wasn't ready to give up or let go. It seemed like the more that we spoke, the more I just wanted to forget all of the bad thing's. I had experienced soo much badness, and all I wanted now was to be happy, even if I meant trying to forgive everyone.

∞∞∞

Over the years Derek had never once spoken or asked me about his best friend Melvin, and neither did I, and he never once apologized to me or showed any remorse for all the terrible things that he did, and said to me.

∞∞∞

I never spoke ill of Andrew to the children I figured that they would eventually see him for the kind of person he was, and they did. Caleb does remember certain things that Andrew said and did. Holly was too young at the time and has no memory of anything.

I am glad that Andrew at least had the decency to shield the kid's from his temper, which always told me one thing. he had never actually lost control, he knew what he was doing every time.

Andrew had never once visited them, and if it wasn't for Steve taking them to see him during the school holidays, then Andrew and his parents would never have seen them at all.

Eventually the children had made the decision to not go and see him anymore, and afterward, Andrew stopped calling.

∞∞∞∞

Andrews mother died a few years ago from Cancer, and Andrews father took to the bottle. They loved the children so much, and they truly were wonderful grandparents. I can't say much for them apart from that, mainly because they were more interested in protecting their son, and family name, than helping me when I needed them, much like my mother who stayed with Derek and protected him and Melvin for simply her own self-preservation.

∞∞∞∞

Eventually, Lucy had children of her own, and my mother and Lucy would make sure that her children were never alone with Derek, knowing how foul-tempered he was, and how rough he could be. I found that to be very ironic indeed.

Chapter Eighty-One

The Broken Road Home...

Steve and I got married in the summer of 2005, in a small beautiful church. I wore an ivory strapless wedding gown, with a plain satin bodice, and a full chiffon skirt encrusted with pearls and diamante sequins. I wore a small ivory pearl tiara with my hair loosely pinned up, with my curls framing my face.

The ceremony was beautiful, and Steve was as handsome as ever. He stood proudly, so tall, dark, and handsome. He was my knight, just like my Nan had said she was working on. I do believe that my Nan sent Steve to me, just as I believed that she was really seeing and holding me on the day I had cried on the end of my bed feeling lost and all alone.

I felt so blessed to be standing beside him, and very lucky that I would get to spend the rest of my life loving him, and being loved in return. The children looked so healthy, and happy. They adored Steve, and Steve adored them.

We went on our honeymoon to Tenerife for a week with Steve's parents, and the children went to stay with Liz and her family. They had an absolute blast. They taught Holly to ride a bike with them, they went fishing, swimming, shopping, and more.

Steve and I snorkeled, cruised beside dolphins, and enjoyed romantic meals, and slow dances.

I cried every single day speaking to the children on the phone because I missed them so much, even Steve got emotional too. We had become a solid little family of three.

∞∞∞

My father was diagnosed with Cancer not long after Steve and I met, and he had been very sick a few months earlier due to receiving radiotherapy treatment. My father, though quite fragile, finally got to walk me down an aisle, and hand me over to a man whom he loved very much, and considered like a son to him. My father held me in his arms and danced with me to "My Girl" which he chose for our father-daughter dance. We smiled, we laughed, we sang!

I loved my father he was a bit like a free-spirited hippy only without the hippy clothes. He was always there for me when I needed or wanted him whether it was me visiting him, or him visiting me a or even by telephone. I learned that he was not one for liking to stay in any one place for very long. He loved everything that life had to offer, whether it was out on the road trucking, sitting in a soundproof booth as a radio DJ, or rolling through beautiful landscapes by motorbike. That was just his way, and he turned up in my life at a time when I needed him the most, and I loved him for sticking around.

My mother and father for the first time in years sat beside each other at the top table, along with Steve's parents and his Uncle as his best man. I did catch my mother staring at my dad in a rather longing way, several times throughout the wedding.

My mother later told me that she" had never gotten over my Dad and that she had, and always would love him." I believed her.

My father went into remission for a time, but then cancer came back and sadly took his life at the age of Fifty Four.

Five years ago Steve and I became kinship carers for our little nephew, from Steve's side of the family. He is a wonderful child, who has special educational needs, a mild form of autism, and ADHD. We were eventually granted a court order by mutual agreement, to have him stay with us until he is eighteen

.

∞∞∞

Caleb has turned into a handsome young man and currently works in the security industry, though his aim is to join the police force, and Holly is currently pregnant with our first Grandchild and when she is ready she is going to University to become a children's nurse.

∞∞∞

I think as a result of my childhood, it made me a better parent. I was very attentive and sensitive to their needs. When it rained we jumped in the puddles, if it was muddy, we ran through it anyway and laughed! I read to them every day, and I taught them many things with excitement and positivity. We baked cakes, and made jelly, we had picnics, and I took them to many different places. I went out of my way to make sure that they had many happy and positive experiences. I told them how much I loved them every single day, no matter what! and eventually.... I was brave enough to move on with them.

I may have been an overbearing and protective mother at times to the point where I have driven them crazy! I would not let them play or have sleepovers at friend's houses unless I had fully vetted the parents. I wouldn't let them play out unless they were right outside the house, and with me watching them constantly.

If we went out anywhere I had to be able to see them at all times, and I would put myself between them and strangers.

I didn't tell the children what happened to me until they were much older, and when I did they understood exactly why I was so over-protective, and of course, then everything made sense to them.

∞∞∞

Our home is full and happy, and I am finally at peace. Steve and I have now been together for fifteen beautiful years. He has loved and raised the children as his very own. He has laughed with them, cried with them, and taught them so many wonderful things.

Steve saved my life by falling in love with me, and my love for him gave me the strength and the courage to break free. My children are the ones who gave me the strength to keep going every day.

Steve is my constant guiding force, umbrella, and shield. Steve and I are like lemming's where one goes, the other follows.

∞∞∞

I look forward to the future with a slightly broken heart where there is always still hope inside of it. Also, I look forward to all the love and happy memories that I make with my family. I try to live my life with kindness and positivity. Maybe one day I will find forgiveness… and if I don't I know everything will be okay anyway.

Epilogue

I often think about the people that have been in my life, the people like Melvin who prey on young girls for their own personal sexual gratification. It was very difficult back then to prosecute people like him without evidence. I had no way to record him, and he was much too clever with me to get himself caught. Melvin and other men like him can be very good manipulators. He portrayed himself to be this caring, happy, helpful person, and he was, but there was also his secret side, which was his, unimaginable lust for young girls. He knew what he was doing was wrong, yet he did it anyway not caring if he tore my life apart, and he did. There were times when I thought about it and I didn't want to live anymore, I didn't want to be touched or loved by anyone. He made me feel dirty, ashamed, and worthless.

I've also thought about Derek, and how he was the sort of person to get angry at the slightest of little things. He was so regimented in how he liked things done, a certain way, and at certain times. He had always disliked loud noises and small children. I frustrated him in the very beginning of his marriage to my mother, I didn't understand why. I realize now that he did those things to me to gain control over me, by beating me into submission. It was as if he was always waiting for me to make the smallest of mistakes, and he would be there ready to pounce. I had already made peace years ago, when I stayed with him to help out with Lucy. I knew then, just as I know now that I was never going to get an apology or answers as to why? I realise now that I don't need it or want it. I am simply just better off leaving him as an example of how not to be a step parent.

∞∞∞

As for my mother who I've thought of constantly over the years. I always struggled to understand why she let Derek beat me, and belittle me, but now I do. My mother is driven by alcohol and insecurity. I think that it was easier for her to turn the other cheek. If she had stood up to him, then she risked either having to leave him, or have Derek divorce her, and my mother would not have wanted either of those things. She had often told me that she wouldn't be able to cope. She had always expressed deep remorse over the years, and she admitted to not being a very good mother and agreed that she was an alcoholic albeit a functioning one. Her family, as well as Lucy, had tried to get her to stop drinking many times over the years, all to no avail.

My mother sat and cried when admitting to me that she knew something was not right with Melvin, but that she couldn't do anything to help me when it all came out, because she was thinking of Lucy and she didn't want to lose Derek, but it wasn't just that, as I later found out it was because she risked losing the house that Derek had bought, and was leaving to Lucy, on the condition that my mother would continue to live there for the rest of her days. My mother would also benefit financially.

She would cry many times asking me how could I ever forgive her? I have never once said that I forgave her, instead I had said "You are my mum. I only have one mum, and everyone makes mistakes." I did accept that she was an alcoholic and that she had her own issues to deal with in her life, making it very difficult for her to help others.

∞∞∞

I have finally made peace with everything negative that has ever happened to me. I will never forget what was done to me. I still struggle every day with forgiveness. I am often flooded by the memories of my past, and I will sit and cry as if my heart is breaking in two. It happens less and less frequently now, but it always leaves me feeling raw... for a while, and then I only have to look at the family that surrounds me, and they give me the strength to keep going, and I love each and every one of them so dearly.

∞∞∞

When I decided to write about my experiences, as a form of therapy I realized that I needed to publish them, because I know that there are many people out there who have been in similar situations to myself and have been ostracised from their own families too like some sort of stigma, or maybe someone has been through some similar experiences as me and were afraid to ever speak out.

I found my happiness, and this was another reason that I wanted to have my writings published, because I don't want anyone to lose hope.

∞∞∞

My mother recently walked out of my life again because I chose to write about my experiences, despite her initial encouragement and support. I am very grateful it wasn't actually her that I was relying on for support, but rather my husband, children, as well as his amazing parents Jane and Joe.

I am happy now for the door to be finally closed. I am now sealing it shut so that it can never be opened ever again.

These disgustingly, terrible things happened to me, not to the perpetrators, and I have lived them, felt them, and have breathed them every single day of my life, and the pain of it will never, ever go away.

My spirit and young body was broken to the point where I wished my young body could have been washed out to sea, or sucked beneath the wheels of a car.

I know that I am better off, and I am not hurt or angry. I feel like I am free of the past, and the constant reminders. I can finally breathe, and write what I needed to.

Acknowledgments

I wish to thank my husband Steve for all your love and support over the last fifteen years. The time and patience you have always given me has been endless. You are forever my best friend, my knight in tinfoil, and my soul mate.

Thank you to my son Caleb and my daughter Holly. You both gave me a reason, as well as the strength every day to keep going. Thank you for all your love and encouragement. I am sorry for being so crazy protective of you both over the years, and thanks for letting me off too! There is nothing more precious than life. I loved you both before I held you in my arms, and now I love you both even more.

Thank you to Steve's mum Jane, Steve's step-father Joe for your amazing support, and love over the years and for rescuing me! I love you both so much, and...

"I wish you both enough"

Thank you to Liz, my beautiful friend, who gave me hope, as well as the loan of her Grandmother's ring!

Thank you, Janice, for your fire! your crazy ideas, and fun antics! I love you both dearly. Always

To the girls at the coffee shop – You know who you are. Thank you for your endless supplies of soy mocha's, humour and kindness! I am ready now for a nice cup of tea...I think. No, actually... I'll stick with Mocha's as I still have more to write.

About the Author

Evie lives in the Lake District, England with her husband, their three children, Tiggy the tabby cat, as well as their little pug/terrier mix Bella. They are a close knit family, and their is never a dull moment in their fun- crazy, happy household.

Evie has a fondness for all animals, especially horses, and she enjoys writing, reading, and handcrafting and nature. She also likes to make her own organic soaps, soy candles and facemasks!

Evie Was diagnosed with Fibromyalgia as well arthritis, and has since had to give up on a lot of things that she previously enjoyed doing, because of these conditions. Evie has since decided to take up writing, and has begun by writing about her life in...

The Broken Road Home.

Evie has almost finished writing her first ever fantasy, fictionromance novel and if you would like to keep tabs on how that one is progressing, or you wish to know more about Evie, then you can visit her website.

You can also contact Evie Gallagher through her website, by following the link below.

Website: www.eviegallagher.com

If you wish to connect with Evie on social media, then you can follow her on Facebook and Instagram, by using the web links below.

Facebook: www.facebook.com/eviegallagher/

Instagram: https://www.instagram.com/eviegauthor/